Ford

and the
American Dream

Founded On Right Decisions

By Clifton Lambreth
with *Mary Calia and Melissa Webb*

D1510779

Daniel Bradley, Inc.

Ford

and the
American Dream

Founded On Right Decisions

By Clifton Lambreth
with Mary Calia and Melissa Webb

Illustrations by Igor Babailov

Ford and the American Dream

Published by
Daniel Bradley, Inc.
Brentwood, TN

Distributed by
Executive Books
206 West Allen Street
Mechanicsburg, PA 17055
717-766-9499   800-233-2665
Fax: 717-766-6565
www.ExecutiveBooks.com

ISBN-13: 978-1-933715-44-5
ISBN-10: 1-933715-44-8

Printed in the United States of America

www.FordBook.com

Chapter Illustrations by Igor Babailov

Contents

Foreword by Paul J. Meyer

MY FORD LOVE AFFAIR

When I was fifteen years old, my brother, Carl Meyer, bought a 1936 Ford Cabriolet convertible. That car was beautiful! One of my greatest teenage memories was when Carl told me I could call that Cabriolet half mine and I could use it when he was not in town—if I would wash it and look after it.

Being behind the wheel of that awesome Ford Cabriolet convertible made me feel as if I were the only one in the world with such a fantastic automobile. It was a beauty! I believed everybody's eyes were on that car when I drove by. I always wanted to park in a special place at school where I could be seen getting out of Carl's Cabriolet. I have often wondered if my big brother ever knew how much it meant to me that he would share a teenage boy's most valuable possession—his car—with his little brother.

Hence, my lifelong romance with 1936 Fords began!

Because of fond memories of those days gone by, I decided to purchase a 1936 Ford of my own. Little did I know that this one purchase would turn into a major hobby! In a few short years I bought just about every model Ford produced in 1936! My Ford collection includes a hearse, a limousine, a three window coupe, and others!

- Before long, I had two twenty car garages filled with 1936 Fords and a large collection of 1936 Ford memorabilia items.

- I have a part-time mechanic, Joe Smith, who takes

WONDERFUL care of these vehicles. We even have our own parts department!

- Each year I add something new to the cars in the museum.

- Every week there is a different car to drive in my home garage.

- About four times a year I invite various community groups and individuals to "Step back in Time" and attend a 1936 Ford car party! Everyone loves to attend!

My Ford love affair is longstanding. And to think that it all began with a big brother's unselfish sharing of his 1936 Ford Cabriolet convertible. Time has only deepened my gratitude to my big brother and my love of Fords!

Thank you, Clifton, for ending your story on a positive note. To me, Ford is as American as apple pie and baseball.

Letter from the Author

Dear Reader,

What you are about to read is *the Ford story* that's never been told! After the threat of the potential bankruptcy of the Ford Motor Company surfaced in December 2006, I decided that I must set about the task of recording in the form of a book the events and decisions that led to that crisis. The threats facing the company have the potential to destroy tens of thousands of employees' and dealers' livelihoods. It is not a single, isolated corporate incident but a representation of the American Dream eroding daily.

As a twenty-plus-year veteran of the Ford Motor Company, I am in the unique position of being able to give—with an unfiltered frankness, and transparency—an interesting perspective on much that has transpired during my tenure.

Upon researching and writing this project, my writing team and I discovered that most of the lessons we learned were universally applicable to other companies as well as those in the automobile industry. There are many land mines to avoid so other companies don't find themselves in the same predicament the Ford Motor Company is in today. We tried to be accurate and truthful. The novel begins with Chapter 11 (symbolic of the Ford Motor Company's present plight on the edge of Chapter 11 bankruptcy) and concludes with Ford's return to greatness. This was written so that the managers of the future will not repeat the mistakes of the past. I realize by writing this book I might be ending my career with Ford. It is not my intent to kick a company while they are down, but I hope to awaken a sleeping giant to return to the greatness it once held.

Clifton Lambreth
Twenty-plus-year veteran of the Ford Motor Company

"It was life on the farm that drove me into devising ways and means to better transportation. I was born on July 30, 1863, on a farm at Dearborn, Michigan, and my earliest recollection is that, considering the results, there was too much work on the place." —Henry Ford

Introduction

The boss was a genius. He was an eccentric. He was no prince in his social attitudes and his politics. But Henry Ford's mark in history is almost unbelievable. If it hadn't been for Henry Ford's drive to create a mass market for cars, America wouldn't have a middle class today. —Lee Iacocca

Christopher Hope's office within the world headquarters of the Ford Motor Company in Dearborn, Michigan, was flooded with the sounds of a hectic workday as usual. Christopher had been with Ford for more than twenty years and had worked his way up the ladder to his current position as vice president of public relations. At the helm of the communications operations for such a corporate giant, he was used to the incessant activity, especially lately.

It had been almost one year now since reports had surfaced mentioning threats of bankruptcy facing the Ford Motor Company. The news had just become worse, with announcements of multibillion-dollar losses and thousands upon thousands of job layoffs. Amazingly, the negative news had only seemed to heighten the American public's fascination with Ford. With every bad news clip came more and more attention. For months Christopher had been fielding requests for information, interviews, and insider scoops from all directions. Christopher handled each request with practiced proficiency, always looking for the positive that he could weave in with the negative. The old adage—"There is no such thing as bad press"—almost seemed to be true.

Christopher made his way around the department as he always did first thing in the morning, checking on his team and making sure everyone had at hand their tasks for the day. It was nearly nine o'clock by the time he finally arrived at his private office where he could gather his thoughts.

Christopher Hope was born in North Carolina and had been relocated with Ford several times before arriving in Dearborn. He was considered to be one of the best and brightest MBA graduates from Western Carolina University, where the company had plucked him from many years ago. He had been a proud member of the Ford family ever since and had done well to live up to the promises of his stellar academic career.

Christopher was a tall man who did his best to keep in good physical condition. He believed in the philosophy of sound mind and sound body. His boyish good looks and unassuming presence were part of his charm. When he entered a room, his larger-than-life smile would disarm even the most vicious adversary. He was known for his quiet strength and optimism. He had a quick wit and sharp analytical abilities that served him well in his communications responsibilities. Christopher had the gift of speech and written communications, and was a natural at them. Keeping up with him was hard, as he had inexhaustible energy for what he felt was his mission in life. His excitement for books was contagious. He loved books—classics and new ones, historical novels, biographies, books of wit and wisdom, and inspirational leadership—and shared them with the people around him. Christopher believed in God, prayer, family, community service, and the American Dream.

Sitting down at his desk, Christopher took his laptop out of his briefcase and checked his e-mail for the second time that day. He always looked through his e-mails at least once during the morning before leaving home. Usually, at least a couple of messages from international publications had fil-tered in during the night. As Christopher glanced through the latest list of incoming messages, one in particular caught his eye. Frank McIntyre, a senior staff reporter for the *Detroit Daily Herald*, had sent him a message letting him know that he would be calling later in the morning to follow up on a conversation they had the day before.

Frank was one of the few reporters whom Christopher trusted. Frank was actually positive in his reporting, certainly an exception to the unspoken rule that Christopher imagined required reporters to constantly go for the negative. Because of his tendency to lean toward the positive, Christopher usually made an extra effort to funnel information to Frank for any stories he was writing or researching.

Christopher tapped out a reply to Frank telling him that he would be available to talk to him in the next hour. As he did with all of his e-mails, he included a quote at the bottom of the message. Christopher's latest emails included a quote by Charles Swindoll that aptly summed up Christopher's outlook on life:

The longer I live, the more important I realize the impact of attitude on life. It is more important than the past, than education, than money, than circumstances, than failures, than successes, than what other people think or say or do. It is more important than appearance, giftedness, or skill. The remarkable thing is we have a choice every day of our lives regarding the attitude we embrace for that day. We cannot change our past. We cannot change the fact that people will act in a certain way. We cannot change the inevitable. The only thing that we can do is play on the one string that we have, and that is our attitude. . . . I'm convinced that life is

10% what happens to me, and 90% how I react to it. And so it is with you. We are in charge of our attitudes.

Christopher felt a responsibility to share his knowledge and inspire others. In a sense, he was a messenger seeking opportunities to bring good news and make the world a better place. For Christopher, the impossible was always possible and dreams were never too big. To him, problems didn't exist; they were only growth opportunities. His view of the world stretched to his role in leadership at the Ford Motor Company. He saw every problem at Ford as an opportunity to improve and excel. Perhaps that was why he was always able to find the positive in any situation.

As a veteran of many of the Ford Motor Company battles such as the Pinto fuel tank recall, the owner dialogue program, the Firestone fiasco, and the Navistar nightmare, Christopher had gained experience and wisdom along the way. He was battle tested.

In contrast to Christopher's long-standing record of Ford loyalty, the company's senior leadership had changed drastically over the years. The leadership had transitioned from car people to big-exec types who seemed to look for megabucks with no real passion for the automobile business. They were hired guns who, like mercenaries, took what they wanted and then bailed out when the going got tough. The result was that the average tenure of top executives had dwindled to five years or less as they jumped to the next treasure ship, much like pirates searching for another ship to plunder.

The transitional nature of Ford's management had created a fear of being fired or transferred, becoming a victim of the right-of-assignment rule, or forced into an early retirement package. The Ford corporate hallways were busy with workers whom Christopher often found were angry and frustrated because no one listened to their Voices. Thus, employees rarely communicated with management or each other about what was really on their minds. The Ford environment was becoming less collegial every day.

It was late March 2007, and a major storm was brewing at the Ford Motor Company. Doomsday, it seemed, was on the horizon. The company was about to experience an earthquake that would rock the planet of Ford. Christopher knew that in the summer months ahead, the United Auto Workers (UAW) contract would be up for review, and the company was bracing for the worst. The UAW, as the major alliance of auto workers, had dominated company policies for years, holding management hostage. Historically, the UAW management team seemed to ignore the environment of shrinking market shares, declining revenues, and diminishing profits as they made their demands. In anticipation of pending negotiations, Ford had leveraged everything it owned to build a multibillion-dollar credit line as a failsafe against anything that might happen.

Impending bankruptcy seemed inevitable. The self-destruction of the Ford Motor Company—an American icon—and the rapid deterioration of the American Dream were unfolding right before Christopher's eyes. In his role as the company's public relations director, he was telling the world that the Ford Motor Company was in great shape, but it certainly wasn't. In fact, leadership seemed to be in a perpetual state of denial. Communications internally and externally functioned in crisis management mode. Business was coming to a standstill with such a reactive and litigation-prevention approach.

In early January, Christopher had announced the news of a $12.7 billion annual loss. This big-billion backlash was the largest loss in the company's history. As critics in the media

15

had pointed out, the Ford Motor Company was losing revenue equivalent to one Mustang every minute!

Christopher was still staring at his computer, troubled by all of these thoughts, when his phone rang.

"Hey, Chris!" It was Tom, Christopher's assistant. "I'm working on the annual press release for next week, and I need your input. What kind of a spin do we want to put on the anniversary of Henry Ford's death this year?"

Christopher paused for a moment. The end of next week marked the sixtieth anniversary of the death of the Ford Motor Company founder, Henry Ford. He had passed away in his home on April 7, 1947, after a bout with pneumonia. A press release celebrating his life and fame needed to be drafted immediately.

"Uh, let me get back to you on that, Tommy," said Christopher. "I'm working through a couple of ideas for that release right now."

In recent years, the anniversary press releases of Henry Ford's death had been pretty standard. This year, however, Christopher felt that more needed to be done. The heritage of Henry Ford was one of the most positive things that the company had going for it. Somehow, Christopher wanted to communicate that message to the public. Henry Ford had founded the automobile industry and, in doing so, had literally taken the country from an agricultural era into an industrial one. He had enabled the establishment of the middle class in America and was the worker's hero. His story was about hope, teamwork, and the American Dream.

This year, times were very tough at the Ford Motor Company. Even those closest to the company—including the shareholders, employees, and dealers—had begun to ask if the company was being true to Henry Ford's vision.

At this crucial moment in the history of the Ford Motor Company, Christopher knew that reminding the public of the company's origins would be more important than ever. Henry Ford had surrounded himself with action-oriented people. He always took a personal interest in his team members and his business. Many referred to the Ford Motor Company as Henry Ford's Motor Company because of his get-it-done attitude. In contrast, at Ford now, there seemed to be too much talk, but not enough action or sense of urgency.

Christopher stood up from his desk and began to pace back and forth. At the moment, he didn't have any new ideas for the press release. He thought that perhaps taking a walk through the Henry Ford Museum might inspire him. Christopher gave a quick look at the weather outside his window. It was an unusually cold and rainy spring day. He picked up his raincoat and was starting out the door when one of the marketing managers came in.

"Hey, how's it going Chris?" asked John. "Got a sec?"

"Sure thing, buddy, sit down. So, how's the chemo coming along?" Christopher inquired. John had been fighting a battle against lymphoma for quite some time.

"Well, the cancer is in remission, but I need more radiation," John answered. "Unfortunately, money is getting tighter all the time, though. It seems like our health insurance just doesn't cover what it used to. Anyway, there's this new treatment that supposedly has great results for cases as aggressive as mine, but it's real pricey."

Christopher's expression turned serious. Management had recently installed cost caps on employees' total health coverage to save money. Then John told him the bad news.

"They let me go today, Chris," said John, lowering his head.

Earlier that morning Christopher had issued a press release about new legislation that would affect retirees. Ironically, that legislation had passed as a result of the scheming of lobbyists and airline company executives, with senators and congressmen in Washington. It would force some of these retirees into Medicaid and Medicare with only a small deductible fund to cover some of their deductibles—certainly not the full coverage Ford promised them when they retired. John and so many others were being abandoned and betrayed by the very company they loyally served. All they were left with was a train wreck of broken trust and broken dreams.

Christopher was devastated. Another key person had boarded the brain-drain train of experienced employees that were being asked to leave Ford through early retirement. Systematically, they were all being replaced by lower-salaried people who were young and energetic and promised enormous potential. The problem was that if you put all the experience of these new hires together, it would amount to no more than a marble rolling down an eight-lane highway—there just wasn't any there. This situation only meant more work for longtime employees who knew something and did something other than inquire about their next promotion and seek personal development. Another high-flyer hire with long-term potential was great, but when would Ford actually realize this potential? The potential of new hires was almost never realized because, most of the time, after Ford financed their MBA, they would leave the company for a more attractive offer. In fact, a high percentage of employees who received a Ford-financed MBA left the company within five years.

"Don't worry, Chris," John said, noticing the grave expression on Christopher's face.

"Everything will work out somehow. I just wanted you to be one of the first to know I am leaving the company."

Christopher paused for a moment and then asked, "Do you mind if we go ahead and say a prayer together right now? I always find that helps even the toughest situations."

John nodded. "That would be great, Chris," he said.

Christopher and John knelt quietly in prayer together.

"My wife and I will continue to pray for you and your family," said Christopher after they had finished praying. "I'll also keep my eyes and ears open for any job opportunities that might be a good fit. Meanwhile, be sure to let me know if there is anything else I can do."

"You bet," said John.

Then John turned and walked back down the hall.

After John had left, Christopher picked up his raincoat and headed out the door. He needed a breath of fresh air, and he still wasn't getting any closer to formulating that press release. He got into his company car and drove toward the Henry Ford Museum, a place he visited often. His visits to the museum were always uplifting and magical. To Christopher, the museum gave credit to ideas that had been born in the minds of the country's greatest, celebrating the God-given gift of human potential that had been realized. It was a true shrine to the doers. In fact, one of Christopher's favorite quotes hung above the large door of the museum. The quote was inscribed on a bronze plaque and read, "The highest use of capital is not to make more money, but to make money to do more for the betterment of life — Henry Ford."

On the way to the museum, dense fog began to set in and visibility was low. Christopher could barely see the entrance to the museum's parking lot. Arriving at the front gates, he was greeted by a museum guard. Christopher flashed his Ford

ID card and, once inside, began to wander aimlessly through the rooms.

There were examples of agricultural equipment, power machinery, and the precursor to the Model T—wagons and horseless carriages and true American ingenuity. Each artifact gave a unique insight into the incredible genius of Henry Ford. Christopher walked through the exhibits featuring trucks and race cars, heroes of the sky, adventures in early flight, and presidential vehicles—all of which were made in America.

How could I capture in words the essence of a man who did so much for our country and for the world? Christopher thought to himself. *If only I could go back in time and meet this man who was one of the greatest people in history.*

Somehow the message of Henry Ford's legacy had to be communicated. The sixtieth-anniversary press release had to send a strong message of focused efforts, hope, and action. Christopher lost track of time as he strolled throughout the museum until he realized it was nearly noon. Then he decided to head back to the office and grab lunch along the way.

On his way back, Christopher came upon detour signs that were twisting and turning him into the rural countryside, in the opposite direction of his office. The detours took him onto dirt roads winding along farm fields. Christopher had not remembered seeing any detour signs before, but assumed they had been placed for the seemingly ceaseless construction that was occurring throughout the city. Soon everything began to look alike, and Christopher became confused. The peaks of the high-rises in the Dearborn area were fading in the distance. He seemed to be heading west. The fog was so thick that he could barely see the road in front of him, and all he could do was follow his own headlights.

Christopher was also getting lost in his thoughts. He was thinking about John and the cruel and devastating early retirement package presented to him at the most crucial time of his life. He thought of all the good people, all the poor decisions, and his job to spin the truth and repackage what was really going on at Ford. Over the past twenty years at Ford, Christopher, like so many others, had tried on numerous occasions and at opportune times to communicate concerns and suggestions for improvement to whoever in top leadership would listen. Each time he and others had spoken up, the response from leadership seemed defensive and negative. Many of the top leaders were overconfident and arrogant in their incompetence.

The sky darkened, and threatening clouds hovered over the horizon. A storm was quickly approaching. Christopher's car began to lose power and slowed down to a halt. He grabbed for his cell phone to call his wife, but there was no signal. Buckets of rain pounded the highway, and a firing squad of hail shot down. The winds gusted, shaking and jolting his car from side to side. Thunder roared, and lightning ripped across the fields. Christopher closed his eyes and held onto the little St. Christopher medal that he kept hanging from his rearview mirror. An Italian lady had given him the medal when he was a little boy traveling in Rome on a family vacation. She said it would always protect him on his future journeys.

Christopher didn't know exactly how long he had been sitting in his car when the winds died down and the storm finally subsided. The sun broke through the clouds, and a beautiful rainbow arched over the highway. He turned the key, but the engine wouldn't start. He turned on his car radio, and the only thing that seemed to be working was one AM channel playing scratchy old melodies from days gone by. Frustrated, Christopher got out of his car and slammed the door. He stood alone on the dirt road, vaguely noticing the cows that were grazing along the meadow and the wildflowers along the roadside. He was lost and disoriented, and everything seemed unfamiliar to him.

Christopher decided to start walking down the road to look for help when a car pulled up next to him, seemingly out of nowhere. Christopher did a double take at what looked like a brand-new, shiny Model T Ford. The ebony-lacquered finish and the chrome shined like polished sterling. The man inside waved and leaned over to the passenger side of the car.

"You look to be in quite a pickle there," the man remarked. "What seems to be the problem?"

"Well, my car went dead in the storm, and then my phone stopped working. The only darn thing that works is one AM radio channel, but it's playing some kind of scratchy old-fashioned music from my grandparents' days," replied Christopher.

The man chuckled. "Can I give you a lift? It's no trouble at all. There's a nice place a piece up the road, and you can ring for help from there," he offered.

"Is your cell phone working?" asked Christopher.

The man seemed perplexed at Christopher's question and then smiled.

"Why don't you just climb on in, young man? I'm sure we can figure something out together."

Christopher looked over at the man in the old Model T Ford. For some reason, he seemed familiar, but he couldn't recall ever having met him. He was an older and distinguished-looking gentleman, tall and of slight stature. He was a handsome man with a striking oval-shaped face of fine-chiseled features. His forehead soared high above kind and inquisitive eyes. He was elegantly dressed in the fashion of the early twentieth century. The man wore a raincoat quite similar to Christopher's and an old-fashioned three-piece suit made from a silklike fabric. Atop his head of fine graying hair sat a stylishly dashing black derby hat. His complexion was somewhat pallid, and he seemed to be trying to keep an annoying cough under control, but was not too terribly concerned by it.

Christopher noticed that the man's radio was also tuned into an AM station, playing the same old-fashioned songs as the AM station played on his car radio.

Admiring the pristine condition of the antique car, Christopher asked with childish awe, "Wow, what a car! Are you an antique car collector?"

"I guess you could say that," replied the man. "I've got plenty more where this came from. Mass production is a wonderful phenomenon!"

"Man, the guys back at the general office would sure like to see one of these in person. We don't make them like this anymore," exclaimed Christopher.

"You're in the automobile business too?" the man inquired.

"Yes. I've been with the Ford Motor Company for over twenty years. You might say it's been my life."

The man turned to Christopher with raised eyebrows and a twinkle in his eye.

"You and I just might have quite a lot to talk about. I've delved in the car business myself. I used to work at the Ford Motor Company years ago. You could say it was my life too. How about you and I have some lunch while we're waiting on someone to help with your car?" the man suggested. "We're almost there."

Christopher looked out at the countryside rolling by. He hadn't realized how far they had driven. Just up ahead was the famous Fairlane Manor, once the home of Henry Ford. The home had been renovated many years ago and was now a popular restaurant and conference center.

The man drove up to the front of the Ford estate and immediately an attendant hustled out to greet them. He ran to open the man's door. After Christopher and the man had climbed out, the attendant went to park the car. They walked through the iron gates of Fairlane Manor and into the grand entrance hall. Christopher noticed that the rooms were oddly empty. He had visited the manor on many occasions, but things looked very different this time.

Maybe they're redecorating or filming a movie or something, thought Christopher.

Then a waiter in a tuxedo quickly appeared. Offering to take their raincoats and Mr. Carman's derby, the waiter neatly placed them in the cloakroom.

"Will you be dining in the private dining hall today, sir?" inquired the waiter.

"Yes, that will be fine, thank you, Albert," the man answered. "And I'd sure appreciate it if you'd see to taking care of my friend's car which got stranded up along Greenfield Village Road, near Miss Molly's farm, after the storm."

The attendant nodded and left the room.

The two men walked down the extensive hallway and into the large dining room where old master paintings and statues adorned the corner ways and walls. They were seated at a formally set table next to a huge stone fireplace. A flamboyant fire burned, spreading a blanket of nostalgic warmth into the dampness of the room. Christopher glanced down at his watch. Although Christopher knew it must be past noon by now, his watch read seven o'clock on the dot. At that moment, the towering grandfather clock in the entry hall began to chime, echoing throughout the manor. On the seventh chime, the clock stopped. A melancholy quiet enveloped Fairlane Manor. Christopher thought that perhaps the tired old clock— and even his own wristwatch—had somehow been affected by the strange storm.

CHAPTER ELEVEN

The Road to Bankruptcy—A Mustang a Minute!

Competition is the great teacher. —*Henry Ford*

"Will it be the usual today, Mr. Carman?" the waiter asked. "You bet," the man replied. "Christopher, I recommend you try some of the fresh vegetables from the greenhouse. There are more than thirty-six varieties grown here at Fairlane Manor."

At that, the waiter pulled a carriage of what seemed like dozens of fresh and cooked vegetables to the side of the table.

"You know what Will Rogers used to say?" asked the man, chuckling. "He used to say that 'an onion can make people cry, but there has never been a vegetable invented to make them laugh!'"

"Will Rogers?" said Christopher, laughing. "I have a book of all his quotes. Why, he was one of the wittiest humorists of his time!"

The man nodded and smiled.

"I also recommend the tomato juice with soybean sauce to start," the man suggested. "The country-style chicken pie made with homegrown soybeans flavored with garlic and dill is one of my favorites. Soybeans are the healthiest food you can eat, young man! You could also try the fresh-out-of-the-oven soybean cookies and soybean sorbet for dessert."

27

"That all sounds great," said Christopher. "I'll have just that."

The waiter nodded and then walked away to prepare their orders.

"Henry Ford was right-on about the value of soybeans. It seemed that at the core of his interests and initiatives was a true desire to help his fellow man. He was a visionary—a man ahead of his times. Why, I was just reading an article the other day about the profound benefits of soy on human health, like heart health, and healthy bones, preventing cancer, lowering cholesterol and other benefits," remarked Christopher.

Mr. Carman raised an eyebrow and winked. "Henry Ford sure knew what he was talking about, didn't he!" exclaimed Mr. Carman with a smile.

"He certainly did," Christopher agreed.

"So, now that I know your name, Mr. Carman, I guess you should know mine," said Christopher, glad that the waiter had taken care of letting him know his rescuer's name. "I'm Christopher Hope."

Christopher reached out his hand to Mr. Carman.

"Pleasure to meet you, Christopher," Mr. Carman replied, shaking his hand. "Actually, I have collected several nicknames over the years. People also like to call me Mr. Farmer and Mr. Inventor. But, since we are both in the automobile business, why don't you just call me Mr. Carman?"

"Great to meet you then as well, Mr. Carman," exclaimed Christopher. "So, do you lunch here often?" he inquired, intrigued and impressed with the formality of the setting and kind hospitality of Mr. Carman.

"As a matter of fact, I do. This is one of my favorite places. It's like home to me," replied Mr. Carman.

"Please tell me more about you," asked Christopher.

"Besides being an antique car collector, what other interests do you pursue? You seem to be such a worldly man. There's something about being here with you at Fairlane Manor. The chance of you coming to my rescue on the road is extraordinary. Maybe it's my destiny to meet you today. I am very lucky and grateful to you, Mr. Carman," said Christopher while searching his own mind for a rational explanation. Mr. Carman smiled warmly.

"There is no such thing as chance, Christopher," replied Mr. Carman. "I believe God is managing fate and that he doesn't need any advice from us. With God in charge, I believe everything will work out for the best in the end. So, what is there to worry about? I don't see myself as a worldly man, but thanks for the compliment. I consider myself a simple man. I appreciate nature and its miracles, and I value hard work. You could say I'm also an amateur astronomer. But most importantly, I am a patriotic American who believes in the Puritan work ethic and the Jeffersonian principles on which this great nation was founded. I believe that opportunity will not overlook a man because he is wearing overalls. I have a passion for engineering and for the automobile. My interests keep me busy, like gardening, car collecting, thinking up new inventions, and traveling. I grew up on a farm not far from here, and I have never gone away from my roots."

Christopher felt at home with his new acquaintance. He was eager to share his thoughts and concerns with him and felt that speaking with him could make a real difference. It appeared this man somehow held the keys to doors he had been hoping to open.

"As a Ford Motor Company man, you may be able to bring me up to speed about the company today, the automobile industry, and the customers' perceptions of both," said Mr. Carman, hopefully. "I have a personal interest, a stake you could say, in knowing the real story about the Ford Motor Company."

"I'm just a small fish in a big pond, sir, but I would appreciate sharing my points of view with you," Christopher answered. "I am the vice president of public relations at the Ford Motor Company. I love my career, and I am also proud to be an American. For many years now, I've had my hand on the pulse of the company's internal and external communications, processing news, communicating and managing it—and *spinning* it. As I see it, the Ford Motor Company is suffering from a series of problems—unfair trade practices, a lack of leadership, a collapse of compensation tied to productivity, bad alliances and deals, overengineering, diversity gone astray, and so many more issues. Recovery, if it occurs, will take awhile.

"This January, we reported an annual loss from 2006 of $12.75 billion. That's $400 per second, $24,100 per minute, $1,450,000 per hour, and $34,795,000 per day! The Ford Motor Company would have done just as well to give every person on planet earth two dollars each last year. Some analysts even estimate that it would have been cheaper for the company to send all of our North American employees to Las Vegas and let them gamble twenty-four hours a day, 365 days of the year. The company would have come out in a better position, financially. The amount of money the company lost in dollar bills would stretch 1.23 million miles. Stacked end to end, 12.75 billion dollar bills could wrap around the world forty-nine times or make two and a half trips to the moon! The amount of loss is incredible!"

Mr. Carman raised his eyebrows. "Las Vegas? Two and a

half trips to the moon? Four hundred dollars a second?" he said, aghast, shaking his head feverishly back and forth. "Why, $400 is about what one Ford automobile cost when they were first produced!" Mr. Carman continued listening intently and seemed to hang on every word.

"The environment of the automotive industry today is domestically overregulated," continued Christopher. "Foreign competitors enjoy lower labor costs, government subsidized programs, and unfair trade balances. Other countries restrict trade. The Ford Motor Company has been fighting in this industry for more than one hundred years. A lot of factors go into the fight and no simple, quick turnaround strategy will ensure success. Things that have led to current conditions are an uneven playing field, subsidized foreign healthcare benefits for our foreign rivals, and the U.S. free-market fend-for-yourself syndrome when competing with foreign companies. To make things worse, the media glorifies Toyota, Honda, and Nissan, making them media darlings. Heck, even the Motor City press seems to favor foreign manufacturers."

"Is that so?" asked Mr. Carman. "Why, in my day, things that were happening at Ford were the biggest news around! I wonder what has changed."

"The media has created a false perception that our company's foreign rivals have a quality advantage," explained Christopher. "In reality, though, the facts say otherwise. The media could help change the perception by just telling the truth. For example, since 1997, the American media has concealed the truth about Toyota's engine sludging concerns in tens of thousands of Toyota products. Some Toyota products of the model years 1997 to 2002 demonstrate sludging that can cause premature engine failure, costing consumers big time. Toyota did not stand behind their products that had this problem, leaving tens of thousands of customers with cars needing expensive repair. Still, they received a pass from the media. In turn, the media has partnered with them to help them get away with defrauding the American public. Toyota agreed last fall to settle the case but seems to deny there was ever a problem. As a matter of fact, Toyota recalled more vehicles than they sold during 2006, but that was hardly even mentioned in the U.S. media. In fact, Honda and several import companies have for years been using odometers that were 4 percent inaccurate, therefore causing the warranties to end prematurely and devaluing their trade-ins. Once again, customers were left holding the bag for expensive repairs and devalued trades. Do you think the media even paid attention to this, even though they've known about it for several years? No! For fear that such news would blemish the import image, the media kept that secret, only to divulge the information when class-action litigation suits began cropping up. The media playing favorites with foreign auto manufacturers has hurt American manufacturers, resulting in lost American jobs. In that way, the American media is a major contributor to the diminishing American workforce."

"The diminishing American workforce?" said Mr. Carman. "Yes, I am aware of this crisis. I can certainly understand your point that the media's favoritism to foreign manufacturers is contributing to this problem. Is the Ford Motor Company doing anything to change this?"

"Well, actually, American auto companies need to do a better job of changing the public's perception on their own because we cannot rely on the U.S. media to do it for us," Christopher answered. "Unfortunately, though, we don't tell the Ford story very well, and when we do, the media doesn't pay attention to it. I don't understand why even the Motor City press would take such joy in bashing the American auto companies upon which so many people in this country depend for their livelihood."

"In my day, foreign manufacturers looked to American companies as examples, as leaders," said Mr. Carman.

"That's true," said Christopher. "Ironically, Ford and Toyota have a long association that stretches back to the 1950s. In fact, Ford allowed managers from Toyota, which was trying to regroup after World War II, to study the operations at its giant Rouge complex in Dearborn. The visits helped Taichi Ohno develop the famed Toyota production system, which emphasizes driving out waste, fostering worker involvement, and making continuous improvements on the factory floor. The very systems that Toyota is renowned for were modeled after good old American Ford's systems.

"Toyota also came to Ford first in the 1980s when it was looking for an American partner with which to open its first plant in the United States. The two companies held brief discussions that could have led to a joint venture to build a version of the midsize Camry for each company. At the time, Ford didn't believe that the partnership would provide any benefit to them, considering the high cost of the venture. So, instead, Toyota entered into a joint venture with GM that recently celebrated its twentieth anniversary.

"Now, there are rumors that Toyota and Ford may work together again as Ford tries to regroup after year-end losses of $12.7 billion worldwide. Toyota, the world's leader in hybrid-electric cars, licenses hybrid technology to Ford, which we use to sell a hybrid version of the Ford Escape, a small sport utility vehicle. Ford has its own hybrid program, but it cut back on hybrid development in 2006 when it decided to place more emphasis on flexible fuel vehicles that can run on gasoline and other types of fuel like ethanol.

"Hybrid technology is just one example of how Ford has become dependent upon foreign manufacturers. Ford buys parts for its hybrid vehicles from Aisin Seiki, a supplier partly owned by Toyota that is part of its global network of parts-making companies. In the past, Ford and AISIN have run into disputes over the number of parts AISIN was willing to make available for Ford vehicles. As a result, Ford has established a relationship where they are highly dependent on Toyota's technology. Ford has been a real contributor to Toyota's success over the years, but hasn't received much in return other than a network of overpriced technology and parts designed to take away any benefit that Ford might receive in the partnership."

"Well, Christopher, is Ford leadership prepared to do something about this codependency?" Mr. Carman asked. "There is no reason for Ford to be tied to anyone. Our people have always been some of the best and brightest in the world."

"Our current CEO, Alan Mulally, is a ray of hope for us on this issue," said Christopher. "He happens to be a student of the Toyota production system and used a form of it on assembly lines at the Boeing Company, where he ran the commercial airplanes division before joining Ford in October of 2006. I believe there is something different about Mulally from his predecessors at Ford—something refreshing and optimistic. He comes across as a common man who is truly interested in the automobile industry and in people, much like Henry Ford was. He seems to be down to earth and dedicated to listening to those around him."

"It sounds like there are many challenges facing the

industry right now," Mr. Carman summated. "I guess some things never change. Competition is the foremost challenge facing any business."

"As a matter of fact, just this morning I received an internal memo further illustrating the uneven playing field between Ford and foreign manufacturers," said Christopher. "The memo details a recent audit of the Ford Motor Company's books which revealed that at least one-third of the cities that Ford has facilities in overcharged 2006 city taxes to the tune of millions of dollars. When Ford asked about recovering these overcharges, most cities indicated that they didn't have the money to reimburse Ford. Furthermore, in many cases Ford was told that if the cities in question did reimburse Ford, they would have to raise property taxes to make up for lost revenue from Ford. Such decisions would require a voters' referendum, taking as long as four years. Meanwhile, some of the same cities that were overcharging Ford were offering foreign manufacturers as much as eight to fifteen years of tax breaks as incentives to bring manufacturing jobs to their area. To cover these tax-free years—you guessed it—the property taxes in these cities are being raised. So, in short, the property taxes paid in some cities are actually subsidizing foreign automobile companies while at the same time overcharging American companies like Ford. This process creates an even more uneven playing field."

"You know, Christopher," said Mr. Carman, "when the automobile industry was created, it opened the door to many competitors. Uneven playing fields aside, in such a highly competitive industry, you have to consistently play at a higher level to win the game. Many companies are not around today because they lost focus and vision and were not held accountable for decisions. Whether you are the leader of a corporation or the leader of a nation, loss is not only measured in terms of dollars, it is measured by human stagnation and the inability to improve the lives of people. It's simple math. A business that makes nothing but money is a poor kind of business. It's not the employer who pays wages—he only handles the money. It is the product that pays the wages. If you are bankrupt in ideas, vision, and product, you will soon be bankrupt in the bank—and the employees, partners, and customers will pay the price. When managers care more about money than doing the right things and providing a great place to work, then the business is doomed to fail."

"I wonder what Henry Ford would think if he were sitting right here with us today," said Christopher in a reflective tone.

Mr. Carman leaned back in his chair and nodded. He had a misty look in his eyes.

Christopher thought that Mr. Carman must be such an admirer of Henry Ford. He dressed and even looked like him. The resemblance was quite remarkable. Christopher brushed off the notion as simply a twinge of nostalgia in light of recent circumstances. In any case, whoever this stranger was, he had hit the nail right on the head. He understood somehow. Christopher took a notepad and pen from his jacket pocket. He suddenly thought that taking notes would be a good idea. The newfound wisdom from this unusual man needed to be recorded.

"Mr. Carman, do you mind if I take notes from our conversation?" Christopher decided to ask. "Next week is the sixtieth anniversary of Henry Ford's death—exactly April seventh. Every year we issue a press release, and I want to make this year's release particularly significant. I want to write about Henry Ford's vision. That's what the American public needs to be reminded of now, more than ever. You seem to think so much the way he did. I thought perhaps you will be able to inspire me in re-creating his message."

At that moment, it grew colder, and the lights began to dim.

Mr. Carman took a neatly starched, cotton handkerchief out of his vest pocket. Christopher noticed two initials embroidered on it but couldn't make them out. Mr. Carman excused himself and put the handkerchief to his mouth and began to cough. His face grew paler. The fire began to slow down its furious pace. Christopher felt a chill straight to his bones and could see a vale of vapor from his own breath.

"Getting cold in here . . . there must be a problem with the heating or electricity," remarked Christopher.

Mr. Carman didn't seem to hear him.

The waiter quickly entered the dining room and brought Mr. Carman a cup of steaming liquid.

"Here, sir, drink this. It will help settle down your cough."

Mr. Carman sipped the hot brew slowly, and his cough began to subside.

"Great stuff this is, soybean tea. They grow these soybeans right here on this estate. You should try some. It'll cure what ails you," said Mr. Carman.

"I'd love a cup," replied Christopher, and Albert went to bring him one. As Christopher drank the tea, he did suddenly feel warmer and stronger. He could definitely understand why Mr. Carman was so fond of soybean products.

"Mr. Carman, I have a great opportunity to tell the real story of what's going on at the company," Christopher continued, suddenly feeling the need to confide in this mysterious stranger. "In addition to the press release, I am working with a reporter at the *Detroit Daily Herald* on a series of stories about issues concerning the future of the Ford Motor Company. I feel compelled to tell the truth, no matter what it might cost me personally. You have years of experience, as a former company man who was with the company when Henry Ford's leadership and vision were still consistent with company truths. Maybe you could help me sort out my thoughts and give me feedback and insights from your perspective of Henry Ford's original vision."

Mr. Carman smiled. "This means a lot to me," he said. "I'd be happy to assist in any way I can. When I was at the company, we had a clear vision that was true to the company's humble beginnings. From what you have just told me, I can see that some—if not all—of that vision has been lost. But there isn't much time. I have only a few days left before I have to travel on. Still, I have a vested interest in the company for many reasons on a personal level that I might tell you more about later. I may even invite some friends of mine to join us who may add value to your search for the truth. Why don't we make lunch here a standing appointment for the next week?"

Christopher quickly agreed to the lunch meetings. Even though he knew he would have to clear his calendar, he did not want to miss any opportunity to share in Mr. Carman's wisdom. He had an uncanny notion that, with Mr. Carman, he was on the right road to finding what he was looking for. Reenergized like a crusader on a noble quest, Christopher found his spirits lifted.

"Albert will take you to your car. I am sure you'll find it's in fine condition now," said Mr. Carman with a slight knowing smile.

Christopher's mouth gaped. He had almost completely forgotten about his car and the mysterious circumstances that had brought him to Fairlane Manor that day.

"Well, that was quick," Christopher recovered. "I expected to be waiting a couple of hours for roadside assistance to get here. Much appreciated. Is there any way I can repay you?"

Mr. Carman smiled, "No, today, this one is on the house."

Albert helped Christopher on with his raincoat.

Then Mr. Carman began to cough.

It was time to go.

"I'll see you tomorrow, same time, same place," Mr. Carman told Christopher, "and remember,

FORD should stand for **F**ocusing **O**n **R**ight **D**etails!"

CHAPTER TEN

Lack of Leadership—Robbing the Future

"Who ought to be boss?" is like "Who ought to be the tenor in the quartet?" Obviously, the man who can sing tenor!
—Henry Ford

A sudden storm had foreshadowed a series of unusual circumstances and a random meeting with a mysterious stranger on a dirt road off the beaten track. The sun was shining brightly, and the sky was blue as far as the eye could see. The detour road signs were gone, and Christopher found himself driving right back on the main highway heading toward Dearborn.

He reached for his phone, which was working now, and dialed his wife's cell number. "Hey honey, it's me. Yeah, I know. Sorry I didn't call you. . . . No, I didn't shut my phone off. That bad storm must have knocked down the power lines. Any damage to the house from the storm? The winds were so strong that my car was pushed to the side of the road, and then I'm not sure what happened after that and then a man drove by out of nowhere and . . ."

But before Christopher could finish telling her everything that had happened that morning, his wife interrupted him.

"Honey, please slow down. What storm are you talking about? The weather in Dearborn has been beautiful all morning—sunny and clear skies. I watched the Weather Channel this morning, and as a matter of fact the forecast called for clear weather across the whole state today and right through the next week! Where are you? Sure you're OK?"

Christopher paused for a moment.

"Yeah, don't worry, I'm OK . . . but I've had an incredible day. I'll tell you all about it later."

He turned on his car radio to his usual FM station, and everything seemed to be back to normal, or was it really? Perhaps the weather was calm now, but Christopher felt the winds of change blowing through Dearborn. Somehow he knew that, after today, things would never be quite the same.

When Christopher arrived back at his office that afternoon, there was a copy of an archived news article on his desk. With it was a note from Frank McIntyre. Christopher cringed, suddenly remembering that he had promised to be available for Frank's call earlier that morning. Frank must have dropped by in person, as he often did when he was working on an important piece. The article which Frank had left on his desk had appeared in the Detroit paper more than a year ago. It was written by Bill Vlasic and Bryce G. Hoffman, and it was entitled "PAINFUL: Ford Slashes 28% of Its Work Force in Sweeping Bid to Save Itself." Christopher remembered the article well—it had caused quite a stir in the higher levels of the Ford Company's leadership. Frank's note read: "Christopher, we need to address the issue of Ford's declining workforce. How is Ford planning to come out of this one?"

Christopher sat down in his chair and began to reread the article. It painted a bleak future for the company—a future that was slowly being realized. It said that the Ford Motor Company was staking its future on the success of a gut-wrenching restructuring of its North American operations that would dramatically downsize the number-two U.S. automaker.

42

It also said that the company was mired in one of the deepest crises in its 102-year history. The company had unveiled its long-awaited Way Forward plan to slash up to thirty thousand manufacturing jobs, cut four thousand salaried employees, and shutter fourteen factories. Bill Ford, chairman and CEO at the time, was quoted saying that these cuts were a painful last resort, and he was deeply mindful of their impact, affecting many lives, many families, and many communities. There was a graph with the article showing the investors' reaction and the stock price falling by half from 2002 to year-end 2005. The predictions seemed to be coming true, like self-fulfilling prophecies.

So much more had happened in one year—more layoffs, more cuts, more debt, and more bad news. Christopher went on the Internet and pulled up the company's three-year stock price history from January 2004 to January 2007. His screen flashed up a similarly bleak chart.

Christopher sat at his desk holding his head in his hands. He printed out the stock chart and then put the press article in his pocket. He would remember to show it to Mr. Carman. He looked at his watch, only a couple of hours remained before the end of the workday. Christopher decided to type up a few of his notes from his earlier meeting with Mr. Carman.

Then, with a glint in his eye, he picked up the phone and called Tom, his public relations assistant. "Hey Tommy, it's me. About the press release, I think we have a handle on this year's spin. Let's title it something to the effect of *This Year Marks the 60th Anniversary of the Death of Henry Ford—A Year Unlike Any Other in the Ford Motor Company's History* and communicate the genius of Henry Ford and the company's commitment to turn things around. Let's throw them a curve ball—positive, positive, positive!"

Then he jotted down a few ideas for the anniversary press release. After an unusually quiet late afternoon, Christopher closed up his office and headed home.

Christopher arrived right on time for the next day's lunch appointment with Mr. Carman. As he pulled up to the front gates of Fairlane Manor, the temperature seemed to be dropping and the winds suddenly began to pick up. Mr. Carman was already there, sitting in a rocking chair reading a newspaper on the front porch. The attendant helped Christopher out of his car. As he did so, Mr. Carman put down his newspaper and waved. Christopher approached the porch. He thought he heard Mr. Carman mumble something to himself like "fascinating, just fascinating!"

"What would that be, Mr. Carman?" Christopher asked.

"Christopher, the possibilities of today's world are endless," remarked Mr. Carman. "You know, in all my life, I cannot discover that anyone knows enough to say definitely what is and what is not possible!"

Upon entering the manor, Mr. Carman and Christopher handed Albert their overcoats. As they walked past the old grandfather clock in the entrance, it chimed seven single tones just as it had the day before. Mr. Carman glanced up at the clock and Christopher glanced down at his wrist watch. The hour hand on his wristwatch was once again stuck at seven. Christopher had replaced the battery only yesterday after visiting Fairlane Manor. The jeweler said his watch was in perfect working order. The appetizing aromas coming from the dining room and the cozy smell of the wood burning in the fireplace soon made Christopher forget about the time.

The table was formally set as it had been the day before. It seemed almost as if a single moment hadn't passed since he had his first meeting with Mr. Carman at Fairlane

Manor. Albert arrived to take their order.

"I'll have the same as usual, Albert," requested Mr. Carman in his polite and unassuming manner, "and please bring me some of that soybean tea—it'll help this nagging cough. Just can't seem to get it under control today."

"And you, sir?" asked Albert.

"The same as Mr. Carman," replied Christopher.

"I like a man who knows what he wants," said Mr. Carman.

Christopher took his notepad and pen from his jacket pocket and placed them on the table in front of him.

"Christopher, I'd really like to hear more about the Ford family," said Mr. Carman. "Have they produced any leaders that my generation would be proud of—people of integrity and those who place the well-being of the common man as the main focus in every leadership decision?"

Christopher reached into his jacket pocket and pulled out the article from the *Detroit Free Press*. He placed them on the table and pointed to the title of the article: "PAINFUL."

"Leadership, you ask?" Christopher retorted. "There has been a lack of leadership at the Ford Motor Company for decades. Look what the former company chairman and CEO Bill Ford had to say to the public last year—a message of doom and hopelessness on the heels of a series of very poor decisions that are finally taking their toll. I found this article on my desk yesterday morning. Frank, the reporter I was telling you about, had left it for me. It seems he wants to address these layoffs in the piece he is working on."

Mr. Carman furrowed his brow as he read through the article and glanced at the graphs. Then he handed them back to Christopher. Mr. Carman could sense that Christopher was upset by the bleak picture the article and graphs painted for

Ford. He decided to offer some wit to lighten the tension.

"You know what Will Rogers used to say: 'We can't all be heroes because somebody has to sit on the curb and clap as they go by!'"

Christopher laughed.

"Christopher, I'm listening," encouraged Mr. Carman. "Tell me more about Ford's lack of leadership in recent years."

Christopher took in a deep breath.

"At the Ford Motor Company, there have been many years of very little accountability. The middle and senior managers have been highly compensated; however, most of their pay is not tied to obtaining results. The same is true for UAW workers. Their compensation is not always tied to results either. Overly dominant senior managers with disdain for both employee and customer input have been steering the company. The management team seems to be more interested in being politically correct than in getting profitable results. There are no perceived rewards for rainmakers. This system has produced managers who just move along without accomplishing much of anything, so they can move up. In turn many of our Ford managers confuse activity with accomplishments and spend half their time telling you what they are going to do and the other half explaining why they didn't do it. Since their compensation is not tied to performance, the necessary accountability is not there."

Christopher paused to see Mr. Carman's reaction to what he had said.

Mr. Carman was markedly distraught.

Christopher was now even more determined to continue.

"Ford's management seems overconfident in its abilities and sometimes lives in a fairy-tale kingdom called Dearborn.

Furthermore, the arrogance of some of our senior managers has limited our effectiveness with our retail partners—the dealers. They seem isolated from the real world at times, and don't value what really happens at the dealership level, especially outside of Michigan. Most of the members of the new superstar management team are great followers that were trained not to rock the boat by challenging top management. So, top management continues to be isolated from the dealers and the retail customers. Also, asking for help or feedback within Ford has been deemed a sign of weakness. It's the emperor-has-no-clothes syndrome where some managers ignore employee involvement and participative management because it's too time consuming and requires that managers must leave their kingdom . . . but it wasn't always this way."

"Tell me more about the sales force, Christopher," Mr. Carman requested. "Are they knowledgeable, and are they given the support they need from company leadership to acquire the skills to do the best job they can and make sure that the customer gets the best product out there for a fair price? Have they been empowered to make the right decisions quickly?"

"It's been a long time since the Ford Motor Company has provided any meaningful sales training to the company or dealership employees," Christopher replied. "Many of the old-timers remember when our selling ability was what led us to market share gains and market leadership. Today's managers, who lack sales training, seem to fall back on a crystal-ball mentality. They constantly look to future products that they hope will make up for their inability to sell the current ones. There's a recurring theme: "Wait until the new products come within the next eighteen months to three years. The new products are going to be dynamite." Ford leaders play this wait-and-see game over and over again, just like an old record stuck in a groove.

"Top management lacked vision and the ability to lead and handed too much of the reigns of the company over to the finance people, who have no sales skills. Their strategy was simply to cut costs at every corner and transfer as many costs as possible to our dealers and suppliers. This created distrust of Ford on behalf of both the dealers and suppliers. Our senior management constantly ignored the backbone of our business: vehicle sales and our partnerships with suppliers and dealers.

"Also, Sarbanes-Oxley regulations and the administrative burdens they place on the decision-making process have destroyed the ability to react quickly to the market. Lack of empowerment because of Sarbanes-Oxley and a litigation prevention strategy are far too often creating paralysis by analysis for our pencil sharpeners in Detroit, who are now responsible for creating reports rather than profits. They can create reports to support any position they want to recommend to senior management."

Christopher sensed Mr. Carman's mood had become worried. He could tell that his questions were far more poignant than they had been the day before. Mr. Carman's cough began to worsen.

"There is a sales skills deficiency in the company and no acknowledgment or recognition of it," Christopher continued. "Rather than build necessary sales skills of employees and franchised dealers, we continue to talk about the new products coming, over and over again, when, in actuality, building sales skills would be much more valuable and produce better results. Management believes Detroit can market their way through this deficiency. This type of thinking is a costly and risky proposition. It amounts to gambling on the next product being a superstar or industry breakthrough. We seem to have a philosophy that salespeople at all levels are born, not developed. Therefore, hiring decisions are made based on likeability and future perceived potential, assuming they will naturally be effective. They have discounted developing the sales ability of employees and dealers to help with recovery. Great salespeople are looked down on and never considered seriously for key positions. In recent years, this has created more and more disconnect between our dealer body and management team."

"It sounds like management at Ford is doing the opposite of what I would have advised," replied Mr. Carman. "They are operating under an unrealistic assessment of their abilities. They are robbing the future, today. Many people think that by hoarding the decision-making power and money, they are gaining safety for themselves. In fact, if money is your only hope for independence, you will never have it. The only real security that a person can have in this world is a reserve of knowledge, experience, and ability. Without these qualities, money is practically useless."

Christopher nodded in agreement.

"I'll give you an example of robbing the future. A former CEO basically robbed our product development," Christopher ventured. "He came from Europe and believed that we were overcompensated in North America and that we paid too much attention to the North American market. He was willing to shift the resources away from the American market, which made up 80 percent of our business! He then shifted the focus of resources to cater to the international market, which then accounted for only less than 20 percent of our earnings and even less of the vehicle sales. Then following his leadership was another guy, also from Europe. He said he wanted the company to become a consumer products company. He positioned himself to become the next GE Jack Welch clone at Ford. He went about spending billions of dollars on dot-coms and other acquisitions that were later sold off for pennies on the dollar. He tried to make Ford a marketing company instead of a manufacturing company. After wasting billions of our dollars, he was paid millions to leave. These top leaders made decisions without regard to the fact that their impact would linger for years. Their careless abandonment of the product cycle, in many cases, would have even longer-term effects.

"Another current leader at Ford has been called a hero for turning around Mazda and making them profitable. But were they really profitable when you considered the amount of original money invested, plus the additional investments over the years? Internally, the Ford Motor Company sometimes uses Ma-and-Pa-Kettle math to determine year-to-year profitability, ignoring capital investment cost."

"Do you think that top executives get paid huge bonuses using this new math you talk about, ignoring the cost of capital investment?" Mr. Carman asked.

"Yes, sir, you bet they do!" exclaimed Christopher. "This is like the U.S. House of Representatives and the Senate, voting, managing, and making decisions on Social Security, knowing full well that it doesn't apply to them. They're under a completely different system. While double standards exist today, the American automobile companies can no longer afford to operate like a governmental entity. At some point, the shareholders will ask how Ford stock can go from seventy dollars per share to seven dollars per share in only a few years while the company is paying out huge salaries and huge bonuses to top executives who have achieved no improvement in real objective results. In addition, the company is paying significant bonuses to some managers who are incompetent as incentive for them to retire early. At the same time, we are also pushing out our best, more successful managers to early retirement and then hiring lower-salary people with virtually no experience. We should be keeping our top performers and paying them well instead of overpaying senior managers who have never performed."

"It appears that the monkeys are running the zoo," Mr. Carman jested.

Christopher laughed. "Sometimes it feels that way."

"Why, you know what Will Rogers used to say," said Mr. Carman with a grin—"'Ancient Rome declined because it had a Senate; now what's going to happen to us with both a Senate and a House?'"

Christopher smiled.

"Here is another example of a project failing miserably and costing millions of dollars. Because of the dot-coms we owned and the Internet, some of the senior managers believed that the Ford Motor Company no longer needed local retail dealers anymore. They had decided to show the Ford dealers how business in the new Internet world should be done. Armed with the arrogance of a wholesale experience and the naïveté and overconfidence that comes from discounting operational expertise, they set out to create the Ford Retail Network (FRN). They went into Salt Lake City and Tulsa and bought out established dealers and replaced the Dealership Management Teams with Ford managers equipped primarily with untested theories, leaving the dealerships loaded down by too many chiefs and not enough Indians. If anyone even hinted at installing reality into this

model, they were reassigned and branded as not team players. They were told, "Trust us. We know what we are doing."
This project disrupted well-established Ford markets and
replaced them with ones that sold about half of the Ford vehicles as the prior dealers had. Eventually, we sold these stores
back to retail dealer organizations for a fraction of what we
paid for them. This is just another example of some of our
Ford managers' net-worth-reduction plan."

Mr. Carman shook his head.

"I believe, Mr. Carman, the root of the lack of leadership
crisis at Ford is in the Ford family having too much control
with 40 percent stock ownership. Although most of the Ford
family is not involved in day-to-day business operations, big
leaders, who might have been attracted to Ford, turned away
from opportunities with the company because they feared that
they would not have full control. As a result, Ford did not
have a lineup of good leaders ready to take the helm when
needed. Bill Ford was asked by the Ford Family to step forward. He could have easily opted out of such a challenge, but
he came forward during a time of crisis for the company and
for the nation. He had the courage to step forward when
nobody else would. For a while, it worked well. As CEO, Bill
Ford was given a honeymoon period. It was expected that it
would take some time for him to adjust to his new position as
CEO. However, he seemed to run out of ammo fast. When he
and others realized the task was too great for his leadership
ability, they were slow to bring in a successor. At the same
time, many key managers left when they didn't fit into his
new philosophy. When it was time to replace Bill Ford as
CEO, the Ford Motor Company had no succession plan in
place to follow.

"Bill Ford became CEO of the company shortly after the

9/11 terrorist attack on the United States had occurred. Life changed not only at the Ford Motor Company, but everywhere in our great country. The government had asked Ford, GM, and Daimler Chrysler to step up and come together with a 0 percent financing offer. They did this at a high cost to the bottom line, but they led onward and kept commerce going. This is representative of the huge impact the American auto industry has on the nation's economy. Did you know that analysts estimate that at least one out of seven people in America are directly or indirectly employed by the automobile industry today?"

Mr. Carman smiled. "Hmm, very impressive. That financing offer was quite a noble effort!"

"I think so as well," agreed Christopher, continuing. "So, as I was saying, when it came time to replace Bill Ford as CEO, the company had no succession plan in place. Desperately in need of finding a qualified new leader, Ford paid $28 million to pull our current CEO, Alan Mulally, away from Boeing. I personally believe him to be an optimist, and he certainly possesses the qualities of a true leader—no arguing there. He is credited with the turnaround of the Commercial Airplanes division of the Boeing company. His fame is based on maintaining 83 percent of the market share in the airplane industry. Analysts say that he has had a terrific record in managing a manufacturing or assembly manufacturing business and also that he has a record of performing, delivering, and cutting costs under very difficult circumstances. Well, in the airplane industry, there are only two real competitors in commercial airlines—Boeing and Airbus. It's not the fierce competition that we face in the automobile industry. New competitors arrive every day, plus our industry is fiercely regulated by the government. Prices are set by the competition and subsidized labor outside the United States. It's a tricky environment we're in and nothing like the aircraft industry. Hopefully, Mulally can transfer his leadership skills to the Ford Motor Company and help pull us out of the spot we're in. We must be hopeful because he's the only hope we have."

"I see," said Mr. Carman. "Well, how long do you think this lack of leadership problem stretches back?"

"In the early 1980s we had leaders that made some tough calls to refresh the products," said Christopher. "They were bright and bold leaders. In my opinion, it was when they retired that problems began. There was no real good succession plan in place to continue their leadership. At the time, our most qualified leader was passed over for personal reasons. Inside the Ford corporate boardroom, in the late '80s, the heart of America was of utmost importance. It was the opinion of many that this leader had too much baggage and his own personal agenda might outweigh the company's best interest. So the company pulled in their second choice to do the job. He was a rough guy with little charisma, but he was willing to do the job. Meanwhile he was up against Lee Iacocca at Chrysler, who had actually been hired by Henry Ford II, but had been let go because he was seen as a threat to the Ford family. Iacocca was a brilliant leader, even though he admittedly had quite an ego. It left us then with a second stringer against a superstar."

"Lack of succession planning has been a downfall for many companies," exclaimed Mr. Carman, struggling to keep his composure. "It is important that there always be a successor in place to share the values and vision of the company."

Then Christopher thought he heard Mr. Carman utter something under his breath, "I told them, I told them. . . ."

"You told who what?" asked Christopher, trying to understand Mr. Carman's last sentence.

"Those who should have listened," replied Mr. Carman.

Mr. Carman was clearly struggling to hold down his frustration, and his cough had worsened. Mr. Carman's breathing was becoming shallow. It was apparent he was trying to keep from breaking into recurring coughing episodes.

Christopher had not realized how emotionally involved Mr. Carman had been in hearing what he had to say. He knew there must be a deeper connection than Mr. Carman had let on.

Albert had returned and was tending to Mr. Carman. He had brought him another dose of the steaming tea.

It was time to go. Christopher stood up to excuse himself and walked toward the cloakroom to fetch his coat.

"I'll see you tomorrow, same time, same place," Mr. Carman said in a rasped voice, "and remember,

FORD should stand for **F**ocusing **O**n **R**ight **D**ecisions!"

CHAPTER NINE

Bewitched by Brand Management!

There is one rule for the industrialist and that is: Make the best quality of goods possible at the lowest cost possible.

—Henry Ford

When Christopher arrived at Fairlane Manor for his next day's lunch meeting with the intriguing and mysterious Mr. Carman, he noticed a magnificently pristine Model T antique car parked right in front of the manor. It was a different model from the one Mr. Carman had rescued him in on the road the other day. The engine was running, and the hood of the impeccable black beauty was propped open. Mr. Carman was bent down beside the car, admiring it.

"Come on over here, young man," Mr. Carman motioned to Christopher when he saw him approaching. "Take a look at a real work of art. Do you know how many American workers were involved in making each part of this engine? It's a finely tuned symphony orchestra, and when it all comes together, what beautiful music it makes! Just listen to it hum. Everyone who drove one of these cars back in my day knew that it was 100 percent reliable and if anything went wrong, it would be fixed quickly and to their satisfaction.

"You must believe in your products and stand behind them, putting your customers first," Mr. Carman explained as he gently closed the hood. "Every time I take a look at this engine, I think of the millions of Americans whose quality of life have been improved by this vehicle. You see, the primary purpose of industry and ingenuity is to serve the common man and to improve living standards for every single person on this earth. If ideas and inventions such as the automobile are born from a scheme to get rich, then we have failed others and ultimately ourselves."

At that moment, Christopher noticed that Mr. Carman was wearing a heavier jacket than usual today. His complexion seemed more pale and his breathing shallower than the last time he had seen him.

"Are you OK?" inquired Christopher, worried about the worsening condition of Mr. Carman's cough.

"Thank you, but I think some warm lunch and a nice hot cup of soybean tea will fix it!" Mr. Carman replied.

Albert was waiting for them inside the entrance and offered to take their coats. Then the two men walked side by side into the dining hall where the splendid fire cast its uncannily warm glow throughout the large room.

"I'll have the usual, Albert," said Mr. Carman, glancing at Christopher, who nodded to Albert, signifying he'd again be having the same as Mr. Carman. He was becoming quite fond himself of the delicious meals and brews he shared at the manor, each featuring soybeans as a main ingredient.

Christopher placed his pen and paper on the table. He didn't want to waste any time, especially since Mr. Carman had an approaching journey abroad in only a few days.

"Christopher, have you ever heard of a snake oil salesman?" Mr. Carman began. "Back in my day, we had such a thing. These characters talked fast and looked sharp. They tried real hard to make you think that, somehow, they knew better than you. They spent a great deal of time and effort trying to convince you to buy into them. In reality, all they really wanted was to take your money, and lots of it."

"I think I know what you mean, Mr. Carman," said Christopher. "In fact, the modern-day snake oil salesmen are called consultants. They charge millions but provide little, if any, helpful advice or strategy. And, by the way, their pay is certainly not tied to results in any way. Brand management consultants, for example, have tricked Ford leaders into making bad decisions that have become roadblocks for Ford along the way. You see, one problem that Ford and other big companies have is that they spend billions on acquisitions or partnerships. Then, they measure executives' and managers' successes based on revenues versus profits. Targets are set, but they basically ignore the cost of original capital investment. All of it seems to tie into brand management. Ford executives are bewitched by the lie of brand management, the twentieth-century version of snake oil.

"For example, Ford invested billions in the purchase of Jaguar as a brand at the urging of brand managers. Then they invested billions more to revamp the product, restructure it, update it, and market it. When evaluating the profitability of the merger, our company's analysts virtually ignored the original investment capital and associated expenses. Unrelated incentives allowed executives to get rich while the company lost big. The real numbers tell a different story. Can you imagine Ford selling around thirty-five thousand Jaguars per year with billions invested? Compare that to selling at least that many Ford cars on one good weekend alone in the United States. Trying to make a profit with billions invested and only approximately 130 dealers and thirty-five thousand units in the entire United States is practically impossible. But the brand managers wanted to keep only a select few dealers, therefore dooming Jaguar to irrevocable financial losses."

"Drawing from our previous conversations, it seems that if profitability was the benchmark used for performance reviews and compensation of managers, their first priority would be to get more franchised dealers in the United States and sell more products," Mr. Carman declared. "Profitability must be defined as revenue minus cost."

Christopher stopped and drew a deep breath. He was always surprised by how well Mr. Carman could drive out the point.

"You cannot ignore initial capital investment and related expenses!" Mr. Carman nearly roared. Color was coming to his cheeks now, even before the soybean tea had been served. "If capital investment figured into accounting of profits, I would think the company would probably double their franchise dealers this year to try and get back their investment or, at least, a positive return on it!"

"Exactly," Christopher exclaimed. "Aston Martin does well in James Bond movies, but as a business model in our portfolio, it's terrible. It's just another example of ego-driven acquisitions. The simple truth is that brand management brings very little to the bottom line. At Ford, it just creates a place where snake oil salesmen, disguised as brand management experts, can hide and be overcompensated."

"Well, what about the warranty plan as it relates to the image of Ford's brand?" Mr. Carman inquired. "When I worked at the company, we set up a warranty plan that put the complete needs of the customer first."

"That's not exactly the case today," replied Christopher. "Ford came out earlier this year and announced an increase to its 36-month/36,000-mile bumper-to-bumper warranty. We added a power train warranty of up to 75,000 miles. Ironically, though, at the same time we were considering adding a 75,000-mile warranty, most of the insiders were recommending that Ford go to a 100,000-mile warranty because that's what Kia and Hyundai had done and GM was sure to do. If we truly believe in our products, shouldn't we have 100,000-mile power-train warranties with a $100 deductible? Instead, Ford announced that we were going with a 75,000-mile warranty, despite almost all recommendations inside to go to 100,000 miles. GM waited thirty days and then came out with a 100,000-mile warranty. So they basically just raised the stakes on us. After being first in so many areas, Ford has been following GM's lead for many years because we lack courageous leadership at the top. But, rather than follow them quickly this time, Ford's brand management gurus advised against it. Ford's marketing team's ego and pride got in the way, and they still have not and will not revamp the warranty policy because they would have to admit they made a mistake."

"The Ford Motor Company is supposedly focused on elevating the brand, but it seems they are neglecting many critical elements that would be meaningful to consumers," Mr. Carman offered. "A warranty is a way for a company to show faith in its own products. Confidence in the quality of one's product is critical when communicating with consumers. What could be more important in branding—if there is such a thing—than communication, right?"

"Brand management is supposedly the application of marketing techniques to a specific product, product line, or brand," Christopher explained. "It seeks to increase the product's perceived value to the customer, thereby increasing brand franchise and brand equity. However, branding should never upstage common sense. Much of the advice from brand managers hasn't worked. For instance, it was so-called brand management consultants who convinced the management team that they should develop a pass key that costs $125—as opposed to the typical key that costs a dollar. The pass key is a device that has a computer chip inside with a key code that is programmed for a certain car. Brand managers claimed that the new key would prevent theft of Ford cars, which would be an important feature to consumers and enhance the brand image. In reality, the device did not prevent car theft. Theft of Ford vehicles did not decrease when we introduced the pass key. The keys turned out to be cost prohibitive and an inconvenience for consumers. For example, if a consumer loses their pass key, they have to buy a new one that costs as much as $125. Then, they have to pay as much as $75 to sync the key to their car. For the average consumer, $200 to replace a lost key is just not practical and certainly not a feature that enhances the Ford brand in their mind."

"Certainly not," agreed Mr. Carman.

"This brand management initiative of recent years even went so far as to push Ford decision makers to eliminate the iconic Ford Oval," Christopher continued. "At the time, the Ford Motor Company Oval was the second most recognizable symbol in the world. My son at the age of four understood the significance of the Ford Oval, and everywhere he saw it, he would say, "That is the company my daddy works for!" But, in the name of brand management, Ford developed the scripted Ford Motor Company logo, even though the branding was already there in the Ford Oval. These so-called experts convinced Ford management that the Ford Oval limited the brand. The new scripted logo was more sophisticated in their minds and would allow marketing of these other premium auto groups under it. All this so they could have something new they could take credit for."

"Well, how did that go over?" Mr. Carman prompted.

"Of course, the change in the logo failed miserably," said Christopher. "Nobody seemed to take into account that we had spent billions of dollars and decades developing the original Ford logo and that it would take billions of dollars to duplicate the recognition we had already gained with it. Disregarding the studies that showed the Ford Oval was the second most recognized corporate symbol in the world, overnight those Ford brand managers threw it out like last week's leftovers and tried to create this new thing."

Mr. Carman interrupted Christopher, breaking into a grin.

"You know what Will Rogers would say about all this brand management?"

"What?" asked Christopher, who was falling right into Mr. Carman's humor trap.

"You know, Will Rogers would say that 'Nothing you can't spell will ever work.'"

Christopher shook his head and smiled at the simple truth in Will Rogers's humor. He continued on.

"Following the advice of the brand management gurus, Ford management also dropped nameplates like Escort and Taurus. The experts said that product names not beginning with 'F' for the Ford line, 'M' for Mercury, and 'E' for SUVs were inconsistent with the desired brand image. The problem with that thinking was that it ignored the millions of dollars spent to build those product names. Both Taurus and Escort were for many years the best-selling vehicles in the world! To create and launch a new brand in the minds of consumers costs millions, if not billions. This capital-intensive marketing strategy also failed. Both replacement products for Escort—the Focus—and for Taurus—the Five Hundred—have produced less than half the sales of their predecessors. This is the kind of thinking and marketing that has led to many years of declining sales."

"Indeed," said Mr. Carman.

"I don't understand how the company could invest hundreds of millions of dollars in name brands like Taurus and Escort for over twenty years and then walk away," said Christopher, clearly frustrated. "We must retain those strong nameplates that have built up so much customer loyalty. Think of the time, energy, and brainpower wasted coming to the conclusion that all of the Ford brand names must start with the letter 'F'. All that time and energy would have been much better invested in developing a car that people want to buy. Such misguided effort is emblematic of years of poor judgment.

"I know this may seem trivial," Christopher continued, "but when you've got a weak car lineup and you yank out one of the props supporting your sales like nameplate recognition, that's poor judgment. Heck, the Taurus was the top-selling car in America from 1992 to 1996. We seem to have a bad habit of trying to launch new names to revive tarnished brands rather than sticking with the good names and improving the vehicles."

"Has Ford decided that nameplates have no meaning or value?" asked Mr. Carman. "They shouldn't be thrown away like old shoes."

Christopher was glad to hear that Mr. Carman understood his concerns. He thought to himself, *Are they going to change the* Mustang *name next? There must be a way to alert upper management to the fact that nobody outside of the brand management offices thinks it's a neat idea to have every other car name start with the same initial as the name of the company. Surely our new boss, Mulally, won't tolerate any of this tomfoolery. He's got a company to save.*

"Brand management also prevents economies of scale,"

said Christopher, moving to other topics within the subject of brand management. "Brand managers advise that each brand should have its own parts. So, instead of having five steering wheels, we have sixty-four. And instead of having three alternators and starters, we have seventy. It's the same case with brake pads, brake discs, and so many other parts. In short, by requiring so many individual parts, brand management causes logistical nightmares for engineering and costs us millions in lost economies of scale. But each part is considered to be essential to the brand, according to these brand managers."

"Why that's preposterous!" shouted Mr. Carman. "The brilliance of our manufacturing system lies in its simplicity. Requiring so many different parts is so unnecessarily inefficient. What are they thinking?"

"Well, it's just that brand management becomes an elixir of sorts," observed Christopher. "It causes otherwise reasonable people to make bad business decisions. They are poor decisions because they are based on the science of brand management, which is a fool's science.

"Ironically, brand management eventually led Ford down a path of consistently communicating the wrong message to the wrong group of consumers. These consultants, some of whom were paid millions to come up with a brand idea, were ignoring the most basic principles of marketing. An example is the implementation of another beauty of an idea called 'The Bold Moves Advertising Campaign,' where the focus of the advertising was on telling ridiculous stories instead of showing our dynamic, fresh, and compelling products. In some cases, the products can speak for themselves without brand managers having to create flashy advertising schemes.

"Another message we were trying to communicate is

'Lincoln Represents American Luxury.' Well, that's good, but they defined the market segment incorrectly based on their mystical research. They began marketing to a consumer group that can't even afford to buy luxury cars. Then they did the same with Mercury. They developed the idea that 'Mercury Is Metro-Cool,' and they defined that part of Ford by what they thought Metro-Cool was. When they listed the characteristics of the individuals that Metro-Cool would appeal to, they were not a group of people who pay their bills on time, are respected in the community, go to church every Sunday, and are active in helping others. They seemed to purposely avoid marketing to the salt of the earth, basically good people that had historically been our most important clientele. The brand management consultants convinced us that the hardworking American public—the same people who have been buying Fords for generations—are not who we want to buy future Fords because they aren't cool enough."

"Why, hard-working, average Americans are exactly who Ford should be marketing to," Mr. Carman pronounced. "What in the world could be wrong with that?"

"I remember raising my hand in a meeting of Ford executives and top managers after a presentation by brand managers on what they thought should be our new target consumer groups," said Christopher. "I tried to remind these brand managers that it is Ford who owns the credit company that is financing these Metro-Cool consumers who are overextended, impulse buyers with a history of not paying for what they buy. It is the Ford Motor Company that would be taking enormous risks to ensure that the cool consumers are the ones driving Fords. I stated that we were forsaking the basic ideals our company was founded on. All of this in the name of brand management!"

"Well, what did they say to that?" Mr. Carman wondered aloud.

"The brand management experts looked at me and said, 'No, we are trying to get the Ford brand associated with the people who are cool, like dot-com and computer geeks, even if they overextend themselves.' They said, 'Times change and we must too.'"

"'Times change'?" Mr. Carman uttered. "What is that for an answer on why Ford should turn away from the very consumers who made the company what it is today?"

"Not to mention that overextending yourself when you are in a credit game will only make you have a bad book of business which will cost big money," said Christopher. "Having to continuously write off bad debt will cause your credit line to go down, limiting credit to creditworthy consumers. But Ford was so bewitched by brand management that they were again suckered in."

"How can this be?" Mr. Carman questioned.

"Well, some of these young brand managers are so savvy," Christopher answered. "They study brand management or get their MBA, read about it and suddenly become brand management experts with no industry experience to build upon. They don't want to build on a company's existing brand because that would not be sexy or get them credit. Then when they want to do something that is different from what makes good sense, they start with their mantra, 'The brand would dictate that we do this, or the brand DNA would suggest that.' It's just like astrology; if you write it general enough, anything could relate to the desired brand DNA.

"So, that's what happened," Christopher concluded. "The science of astrological brand management led us to sponsor certain events, launch expensive campaigns, and do countless other things all to line up with the brand. For example, Ford spent millions endorsing a professional golfer on the PGA Tour, but was that really money well spent? When you look at the interests of Ford customers, we probably would have been wiser to spend those millions targeting the outdoor crowd of hunters, fishermen, and rodeo-goers. Our research clearly showed that we should have showcased the Lincoln brand on the PGA tour instead. In the end, none of this produced sales or increased market share. In fact, we have consistently lost market share and profitability while involved in this brand management initiative.

"What brand management does is it allows these consultants to bring in friends of theirs—cronies who are other so-called brand experts and advertising executives—and overpay them with, again, no accountability for the impact of sales. If they were paid for results, they would all have had to return millions, if not billions to the Ford Motor Company—instead of taking home their millions in compensation."

"Unbelievable!" said Mr. Carman. "All the while, Ford is paying for this foolishness?"

"They are paying big time," said Christopher. "Many of these brand managers are privy to company expense accounts and myriad other plush benefits. One time, they hired a guy who used to work for a high-end foreign luxury brand to come in and set up a premier auto group based on his vast knowledge of brand management. In order to do so, he convinced the company that he had to conduct research on American luxury—all at Ford's expense, of course. So, on the Ford Motor Company's credit card, he stayed in luxury hotels and luxury resorts so that he could 'experience American luxury' and know how to define what Lincoln and other premier groups should be. He was literally jet-setting all around the country, staying in the best resorts, eating the best meals, and running up a bunch of frivolous expenses. As it turns out, he was not even completing his monthly travel expense reports. There was absolutely no accountability for him. He was a free agent doing exactly what he wanted to do. This guy was so reckless that one day, while surfing on the Internet, he managed to pick up a virus and send it through a bulk email to all U.S. Ford computers, shutting them all down for almost two days! It cost us millions in lost productivity. A red flag was finally raised when accounting noticed that he hadn't submitted any expense reports after he asked to up his credit limit on his corporate credit card. That's when they realized that this bad decision-maker employee was running around the country spending money like there was no tomorrow."

Mr. Carman just stared. Christopher imagined that in his generation, such bold trickery was surely unheard of.

"I agree that it is good to understand your customer," Christopher continued. "However, it is another thing to create a customer niche and then try to develop a brand around someone who isn't buying or likely never will buy your products. Trying to design a car to go after a specific brand image of a customer is backwards engineering and will only cause you to fail. Ford should have learned that from the Edsel car. The Edsel is a world-famous vehicle line that every market research company in the world has done case studies on. In developing the Edsel, Ford asked people what they wanted and threw it all in one car, thinking we would have the cure-all. It failed miserably because the cost was prohibitive. We had to price accordingly in order to have all of these assets.

"You see, consultants prey on this science of brand management. They hover around like scavengers who come in and offer you brand management advice for millions of dollars that never justifies itself in vehicle sales. Ford was sold snake oil."

"Well, as I said, we had snake oil salesmen in my day, too," Mr. Carman said. "Every week, we would have a snake oil salesman come in promising that if we would use their motor oil, the engine would never wear out, or if we would use their fuel, we could double or triple the fuel economy of our vehicles. The fact is, no product existed that could do any of those things and we knew it. I guess they didn't learn, did they? Yeah, we had brand managers in my time—I've met those guys before. We ran them out of the company once, and it sounds like that needs to happen again.

"You know," Mr. Carman continued, "the Ford Motor Company was built on the ability to maximize profits through the establishment of mass-production systems and intellectual property rights. Ford dampened the success of others who were focused on inventing premium vehicles for the rich. A good friend of mine once said that he wouldn't want to invent anything that wouldn't sell, and I agree. 'Sales are proof of utility and utility is success,' my friend always said. A misconception by many is that the money value of an invention constitutes the reward to its inventor. But I always found my greatest pleasure, and so my reward, in the work that preceded what the world calls success because I enjoyed the work itself more than the reward. I never did anything by accident, nor did any of my inventions for the company come by accident—they came by work. Another thing I've learned is that success does not bring happiness, but rather, happiness brings success. The three great essentials to achieving anything worthwhile are hard work, dedication, and common sense. Remember to remind them, Christopher, that bad alliances and bad ideas mathematically equal waste—and waste is worse than loss. The time is coming when every person who lays claim to ability will keep the question of waste before them constantly. The scope of thrift is limitless."

At that very moment, the old grandfather clock chimed seven times. Christopher had not worn a watch today. He had taken it back to the shop to be repaired. *They really should fix that old clock*, he thought to himself.

Mr. Carman stood up and glanced thoughtfully at the old grandfather clock. His cough began to act up again. The room became cold and damp and the lights flickered.

It was time to go.

"Mr. Carman," Christopher said, standing up to leave, "thank you for hearing me out and listening to my views on brand management and the detriment it has been to the Ford Motor Company. I don't know why, but I can't help feeling like you really understand what we are going through. I have this feeling that you will be able to help us."

Mr. Carman smiled patiently and walked with Christopher to the entrance. Christopher fetched his raincoat from the cloakroom. Then Mr. Carman waved good-bye and said, "I'll see you tomorrow, then, same time, same place, and remember,

FORD should stand for **F**ocusing **O**n **R**ealistic **D**ecisions!"

Chapter Eight

Engineered to Fail

A market is never saturated with a good product, but it is very quickly saturated with a bad one. —Henry Ford

The next day, when Christopher arrived at Fairlane Manor to meet with Mr. Carman, he noticed yet another model antique car parked in front of the estate. This time, Mr. Carman was in the driver's seat, and Christopher could see the silhouette of someone seated next to him. Christopher pulled up in front of the antique Model T Ford and called out to Mr. Carman.

"Wow, just how many of these little collectibles do you have?" exclaimed Christopher. "This one looks brand-new!"

"It is new, Christopher!" Mr. Carman replied. "I thought that today since the weather is a bit better, we might ride around the grounds. Albert has even prepared us a picnic lunch. I also invited an old friend of mine to join in our conversation today, and I thought it appropriate—for old times' sake—that we eat outdoors together. My friend and I used to go on camping trips. Great fun it was—building dams on small streams and examining old mills for a calculation of the power output!" Mr. Carman recollected.

Christopher was always amazed by Mr. Carman's vast variety of interests. He had noticed that the weather today was somewhat better. Sunlight had broken through the dark clouds which always seemed to hover over Fairlane Manor, and the warm rays were burning off some patches of fog. *It would be nice to enjoy the afternoon outside*, he thought.

"Well, you know what they say," Christopher laughed. "There are only two seasons in Michigan—winter and the Fourth of July! I guess today is more like the Fourth of July! We should enjoy the weather while we can."

Christopher could see that the man in the passenger's seat was laughing with Mr. Carman at Christopher's joke. The man gave a friendly wave to Christopher.

"Nice to meet you, sir," said Christopher.

The man didn't seem to hear him.

"Speak up, Christopher. Talk right into his ear if you can," Mr. Carman directed. "He's been hard of hearing for years!"

Mr. Carman smiled.

Christopher leaned forward toward the man.

"Nice to meet you, sir," he called out more loudly this time.

The man turned to Christopher and returned the smile.

"It's a pleasure to meet you too," he replied.

Christopher didn't know his name nor did he venture to ask. Besides, if Mr. Carman had wanted him to know it, he would have told him. Mr. Carman was a man of many peculiar confidences, Christopher had learned.

"Park your vehicle and hop on in, young man," Mr. Carman called to Christopher, who was pulling up next to him.

Mr. Carman's mood today was playful. Being in the company of his old friend seemed to be helping him forget about his worries and his nagging cough. He was bundled up for the outdoors, wearing a heavy woolen scarf wrapped securely around his neck to keep him extra warm.

Christopher studied the man in the passenger seat of the car as they drove along the garden roads of Fairlane Manor. He was a distinguished and elegant-looking gentleman. He wore a three-piece vested costume of high fashion. A perky black bow tie sat neatly atop his white, starched, round-collared shirt, and Christopher noticed the gold initialed cufflinks peeking out of his coat sleeves. *Maybe these guys are members of an antique car club of sorts*, thought Christopher.

Mr. Carman's friend had a mass of snowy-white hair which was combed to the side of his high forehead. He had an air of high class and wit about him. His bushy dark eyebrows framed ice blue eyes full of fire and passion. The man sat contently beside his friend, looking out at the countryside and seeming to enjoy the ride as Mr. Carman drove his car down the winding roads of the estate.

They arrived at a small pond. There, next to a field of what looked like newly planted vegetables, were a table and chairs carved in stone. The table was set, and plates of food were already waiting for them. Christopher could see the familiar steam rising from the cups of soybean tea. He watched as Mr. Carman walked over to his friend and put his arm around his shoulder. The two men began to reminisce about their past.

"Remember the convention in Manhattan Beach in New York?" asked Mr. Carman.

"Why, of course I do," his friend answered. "Yes, it was quite a banquet."

"And do you remember the time we first met? You marveled at our self-contained car that carried its own power plant. Why, you banged your fist down on the table, ecstatic about that gas car we made!" recounted Mr. Carman.

His friend let out a jolly laugh.

"That bang on the table was worth worlds to me," continued Mr. Carman. "No man up to then had given me any encouragement. I had hoped that I was headed right. Sometimes I knew that I was, sometimes I only wondered, but here, all at once and out of a clear sky, the greatest inventive genius in the world—you—had given me complete approval. I will never forget those words."

The man smiled warmly at Mr. Carman.

"And do you remember the crowds which lined thirty miles of Detroit streets on the fiftieth anniversary party for the institute?" reminded the man. "Your company sent in seven railroad cars of New Jersey soil for the reenactment of my company's first successful invention in our laboratories."

Mr. Carman nodded and smiled.

"You even tried to get an old elm tree that stood near the lab door, but had to settle for a cutting of the old tree planted in the same spot," added the man.

The two men chuckled and laughed as Christopher stood to the side, leaning on the hood of the Model T. He wanted to leave the two buddies alone to themselves and not to appear to be eavesdropping on their conversation. It seemed to be a very special moment for Mr. Carman, and Christopher was feeling happy for him.

"The whole nation turned their lights on that night—in honor of the anniversary celebration," remarked Mr. Carman.

"They sure did," replied the man.

As the two men spoke together, a warm light of memory surrounded them. Mr. Carman seemed years younger today. Their energy was electrifying. Mr. Carman's friend took a cigar out of his vest pocket and lit it and puffed away. Mr. Carman took sips of his favorite drink, soybean tea. The mood was light and peaceful.

Christopher had stepped into a world where the line between dreams and reality, fiction and nonfiction coincided. He felt like he was walking on a moving ramp toward a light at the end of a long dark tunnel.

Albert arrived with a fresh pot of tea, and they all

sat down at the picnic table for lunch.

Christopher sat down on the cold stone bench. He took his pen and paper from his raincoat and placed them on the table, ready to write.

They got down to business as Mr. Carman introduced the conversation of the day.

"Engineering is one of the most exciting and important processes of any company. Why, without engineering, realizing an inventor's creation would be impossible," Mr. Carman remarked.

Mr. Carman's friend nodded in agreement.

"See that automobile over there?" Mr. Carman continued. "The Model T was one of the most important and successful automobiles ever engineered. Christopher, did you know that the Model T was the chief instrument of one of the greatest and most rapid changes in the lives of the common people in history, and that it affected this change in less than two decades?"

Christopher smiled. He had never thought of it that way before.

"After the Model T came along, farmers were no longer isolated on remote farms," Mr. Carman explained. "Reliance on horses for transportation disappeared so rapidly that the transfer of acreage from hay to other crops caused an agricultural revolution. In turn, the automobile became the main prop of the American economy and a stimulant to urbanization. Cities spread outward, creating suburbs and housing developments. Soon came the building of the finest highway system in the world.

"The original Ford cars were built for the great multitude. In the first nineteen years of its existence, the Ford Motor Company sold more than 15 million cars in the United States, almost 1 million in Canada, and 250,000 in Great Britain: a production total amounting to half the auto output of the world. By then, the motor age had arrived. The car was made to be the ordinary man's utility rather than the rich man's luxury, so millions could go wherever they pleased."

"That was part of Henry Ford's vision and what transitioned our society from the agricultural era to the industrial era," Christopher contributed. "Later, because of the development of the automobile, the U.S. highway system was created, connecting every state in the United States except Alaska and Hawaii."

Mr. Carman's friend listened intently, nodding his head in agreement.

"In my engineering days," Mr. Carman recalled, "I was always of the mentality myself of not merely achieving increased capacity, but complete self-sufficiency. The making of the Model T is a great example of this. World War I had many shortages and price increases which demonstrated the need to control raw materials. Wheels, tires, upholstery, and a number of accessories were purchased from other suppliers. As the Model T production increased, these smaller operations had to speed their output, and many had to install their own assembly lines. It had become impossible to coordinate production and shipment so that each product would arrive at the right place and at the right time. At first, the company had tried accumulating large inventories to prevent delays or stoppages of the assembly line, but it was soon realized that stockpiling was wasted capital. Instead, the company took up the idea of extending movement to inventories as well as to production. At that time, it was thought that manufacturing began the moment the raw material was separated from the earth and continued until the finished product was delivered to the consumer. So the company built a plant in River Rouge that embodied the idea of an integrated operation, encompassing production, assembly, and transportation. In pursuit of a true vertical integration model, the company purchased a railroad, acquired control of sixteen coal mines and about seven hundred thousand acres of timberland. They also built a sawmill and acquired a fleet of Great Lakes freighters to bring ore from Lake Superior mines as well as a glassworks. Imagine that!

"The move from Highland Park to the completed River Rouge plant was accomplished in 1927," Mr. Carman reflected. "At eight o'clock every morning, just enough ore for the day would arrive on a Ford freighter from Ford mines in Michigan and Minnesota and would be transferred by conveyor to the blast furnaces. Then, it was transformed into steel with heat supplied by coal from Ford mines in Kentucky. It would continue on through the foundry molds and stamping mills until, exactly twenty-eight hours after its arrival as ore, the material would emerge as a finished automobile. Similar systems handled lumber for floorboards, rubber for tires, and so on. At the height of its success, the company's holdings stretched from the iron mines of northern Michigan to the jungles of Brazil and among thirty-three countries around the globe. Most remarkably, not one cent had been borrowed to pay for any of it. It was all built out of profits from the Model T."

"That's amazing," Christopher said. "I think sometimes we forget how incredibly integrated Ford's manufacturing process was at one time."

"Well, I have to say that in the later years that ensued, on the heels of such unprecedented success, company leadership, having absolute control of the company, began driving out subordinates with contrary opinions," said Mr. Carman. "In some ways, success can lead to complacency. With such intolerance of varying ideas, the company experienced a decline. Ford was surpassed by other automobile manufacturers who were offering such innovative features as conventional gearshifts—Ford held out for its own planetary gear transmission; hydraulic brakes—Ford continued with mechanical ones; six- and eight-cylinder engines—the Model T had a four-cylinder engine; and a choice of colors—from 1914 every Model T was painted black. Finally, the company became convinced that the market had changed and was demanding more than a purely utilitarian vehicle. Ford shut down the plants for five months to retool."

"Then in December 1927, the company introduced the Model A. It enjoyed solid but not spectacular success. The Model A was outsold by General Motors' Chevrolet and Chrysler's Plymouth and was eventually discontinued in 1931. Despite the introduction of the Ford V-8 in 1932, by 1936 Ford Motor Company was third in the industry. We had lost our competitive edge.

"Back to the Ford Motor Company today," Mr. Carman continued, "how is the company optimizing its engineering capabilities? After all, Ford's engineering rests on a foundation of almost a century of solid technical and business experience."

"Well," Christopher began, caught a little off guard, "there's only one solution for the engineering problems facing the Ford Motor Company today, and that is to build all vehicles worldwide to North American standards and not sign a contract with the union that restricts the company from importing and exporting any products."

"That sounds sensible," Mr. Carman commented. "Do you see any other opportunities for improvement?"

"Well, we haven't used economies of scale to the fullest extent like we could if we were looking at the global picture and putting it all in perspective," replied Christopher. "Currently, we allow each engineering team, each vehicle team, each commodity team, and each platform team to optimize their vehicle independently in style and in part content. Each product is then designed and built without regard to other product lines, and in the end, that just doesn't work. There has to be accountability upward and somebody who says, 'You can optimize your vehicle, but here's the menu to choose from.' Without this accountability, we've over-engineered many of our cars. As a result, we have eighty-four different alternators where we really only need a few, and we have over fifty-four steering wheels, when Toyota and Nissan have just a handful."

"Is that so?" Mr. Carman said thoughtfully. "It seems the company has other priorities than simply ensuring engineering efficiency. Unfortunately, though, whatever you put the most focus toward tends to increase. If the Ford Motor Company is so concerned with allowing each team its individuality, that feeling of independence will only increase in a direction further and further away from engineering efficiency and economies of scale."

Christopher commented, "While allowing engineers creative freedom to create whatever they want may work on cable reality shows like *Pimp My Ride* or *West Coast Choppers*, it is a recipe for disaster in the automobile assembly business. You must manage your costs and improve the serviceability. I always think those vehicles on those shows are so cool, but you never see what happens when those one-of-a-kind gadgets go bad or break."

"'Pimp my ride'?" asked Mr. Carman, bewildered.

Mr. Carman's friend also looked perplexed.

"That's a popular reality TV show," Christopher replied, but by the confused look on the gentlemen's faces, Christopher surmised that neither watched much cable television. Since explaining that further might take the conversation off track and time was of the essence, he decided to leave it at that.

"As I see it," Christopher continued, "there's too much complexity, and this limits our economies of scale in purchasing and makes serviceability a nightmare. Servicing dealers have to stock too many parts or risk causing customer delays in having their vehicles repaired if something goes wrong."

Mr. Carman's friend turned to Christopher and said, "The engineering departments must share best practices or lessons learned with other teams," he suggested. "Everyone should be aiming for the same goal, which is making the best products possible. Sharing information within the company is the best way to achieve that."

"Right you are!" exclaimed Mr. Carman.

"Today, there's simply very little engineering of the engineering department," explained Christopher. "Everyone in engineering is a Lone Ranger. Platform managers are hiding their secrets from everyone else because they're trying to get promoted. They seem self-serving, trying to maximize their own careers. The mentality is, 'If I come with the best product, and it's really cool, then I'll be in line for the next job as VP of engineering!' So they don't talk or share. That could be solved with a restructuring of compensation that provides incentives for team sharing.

"As I mentioned before, currently the optimization of every product that will be part of our future product line minimizes the ability to leverage our economies of scale. Engineers have a tendency to grab the latest technology sometimes even before it's adequately tested. And since parts are not uniform across all the products, as a Ford customer you may get in one product and the gas tank is on the left side when in the next product, it's on the right. We probably have forty-some gas tanks for different products as well."

Mr. Carman shook his head and seemed astonished at the numbers Christopher was spouting.

"If Ford is going to keep making over a million vehicles per year, we have to have some common platforms and common parts so we can buy at a discounted rate using economies of scale. Toyota has been doing this for years. They actually continue using the same platforms as they update a model from year to year and simply tweak it as new, tested technology becomes available. In other words, if it's working, they don't break it. When you get inside a Toyota, it's simple and consistent. What people like is that they don't ever have to worry about it breaking down because its limited technology has already been tested and been proven across all their products. They also keep their cost structure down because they are using the same parts in multiple vehicles.

"The Ford Motor Company seems to look at it the other way around; if it isn't broke, break it. Each year, they redo entire models with new parts, which costs a lot and makes it harder to service. It's weird. This whole engineering problem creates issues in mass parts production and dealer complexity in servicing the vehicles throughout the United States or around the world. As I mentioned, the dealer then has to stock so many parts. If there was accountability of the engineering departments for the quality problems or lost profits, I don't think we'd have so many parts."

"I'd think not," agreed Mr. Carman.

"Another problem in engineering is in the use of U.S. standards for our vehicles," Christopher explained. "U.S. manufacturing standards are higher than standards anywhere else in the world. That's the condition of the market, and it is fine. Importantly, Toyota builds to U.S. standards all across the world so they can move their products around. Ford only builds North American products to U.S. standards and builds sub–U.S. standard products all across the world in Australia, China, Japan, and other countries. They build to different platform levels to accomplish minimum standards for that region. So, if a product is successful elsewhere, we can't bring it in to the United States because the costs to bring it up to U.S. standards retroactively would be prohibitive. If we built American standards into the costs when originally manufacturing all of our products, the cost difference would be insignificant and we could transfer successful products across all markets. Economies of scale would easily offset upgrades.

"One significant reason that we don't transfer great products from other countries into the United States is the UAW. The UAW has a fit. We brought in a car called the Merkur years ago. It was a great product, a German car. The UAW went crazy. Today, we have the KA in Europe, which is a dynamite small car. We could use it here in America, as an entry level small car that we badly need. Why don't we have such an entry level car in the United States now? We already have it designed in Europe. It's ready to go, but we can't bring it to the United States because the UAW would probably threaten to walk out. They would walk off the lines and shut the company down. And, you guessed it—the KA is not engineered to U.S. standards anyway. So, to develop the KA in the United States, we have to get on our three- or four-year product development cycle to design and build a separate North American version."

"Let me get this straight, Christopher," said Mr. Carman, trying to digest all that Christopher was suggesting. "From what you're telling me, the Ford Motor Company currently has no common platforms built to U.S. standards and no accountability installed in the engineering department. And leadership has turned a blind eye to insider competition in Ford's foreign markets. Budgets have to be respected.

Leadership has to lead. It sounds like mutiny on the bounty on the high seas! Right now, they're engineered to fail!"

"Nobody holds them responsible. On the contrary, they get promoted for doing things the way they do," Christopher replied. "As your friend wisely said, there needs to be a sharing of ideas. There needs to be collaboration and cooperative efforts. Our engineers have got to be rewarded for being team players, not for being the Lone Rangers. Right now, the compensation plan does not support that kind of model as we have the Lone Ranger engineering approach, where if you come out with the best deal and nobody else finds out till you get it out, then we promote you. There's going to have to be a whole overhauling of the engineering department, from one end to the other."

"It seems like engineering isn't listening to the voice of the customer and has a preconceived notion of what's important," concluded Mr. Carman. "What do our dealer partners think about this process?"

"Ford dealer partners are the most loyal in the world," explained Christopher. "However, they are growing more frustrated every day. They can see that the Ford management doesn't listen very well to the voice of the customer, the dealer, or anyone else. And most of our engineering staff is a generation or two behind the people who are buying the vehicles. I remember being in an XL2000 meeting once with the top fifty dealers in the United States. One of them asked the Ford VP of engineering why the company didn't offer more convertibles. The VP answered him by telling him that customers didn't want them. The Ford dealers adamantly disagreed. Our dealers are face-to-face with our customers every day! Why would engineering assume that they know what the customers want better than our dealers?"

"You cannot lose touch with the customers," said Mr. Carman. "Being in touch with the customer on a regular basis allows your dealers to understand which direction to go with products, service, and everything in between. With such a large dealer network, it seems to me that Ford should be more in tune with customers than anyone."

"That's the problem. We basically ignore our dealers," Christopher replied. "There is a complete disconnection between the engineering community and our distributors, which are the dealers who sell our vehicles, stock the parts, and take care of the end user. Here is a hypothetical example: the industry standard for engineering a certain vehicle might be eight out of ten. But, if an engineer is full of himself and full of his future with the Ford Motor Company, he might decide that, for the vehicle he is working on, the standard is going to be a nine. Even though every vehicle in the world is built to an eight standard, because of Ford's engineering prac-tices, this engineer can arbitrarily decide that it's going to be a nine. This decision instantly negates using any common platforms or any common parts. Special parts have to be developed which meet the Ford spec, which is already above everything else. And so, as a result of this unnecessary overengineering, Ford prices itself out of the market. The rea-son Ford has priced itself out of the market is that the eight standard requires a five-dollar part, but the nine standard requires a nine-dollar part. Those costs must be built in to the price. A vehicle is made up of fifteen thousand parts on aver-age. The parts are made from a variety of materials such as plastics and metals to space-age materials. The parts go through a rigorous production process where they are bonded, welded, screwed, and riveted together. Then, when the pro-duction process is complete, the parts have to be able to work in temperatures below freezing and above one hundred degrees.

"Without engineering commonality into this process,

there is no discipline and you can see where costs can run amok quickly," continued Christopher. "If our manufacturing process is 90 percent accurate, there is still a potential failure of 150 parts. Even if we are 99.9 percent accurate, there is still a potential failure of fifteen parts. That is why engineering is critical to achieving a positive customer ownership experience."

Mr. Carman was visibly disturbed by what Christopher had shared with him. He fidgeted around in his chair and tried to keep from coughing. Albert appeared and brought the group some more soybean tea. Mr. Carman's friend frowned and shook his head from side to side.

"The best example of this," continued Christopher, "is the Ford Contour and Mercury Mystique, which inside Ford we call the Ford 'mistake.' They tried to force a new segment that was somewhere between an Escort and a Taurus, but that cost more than a Taurus. It was an overengineered product that should have cost a billion dollars to produce, and instead it cost several billion! Employees who were on these teams were rewarded and promoted instead of being held accountable for the cost overage. Six billion dollars—that's six times what it was originally estimated to cost! Even so, they were not held accountable. They built the Edsel—a product that nobody wanted. The Taurus and the Escort were very highly successful vehicles leading their class at that time—among the top five sellers in the world. Imagine trying to create a product between two of the top five sellers in the world that was going to cost 30 percent more than either of them. It was a 'we're-going-to-sell-you-less-for-more' mentality. It was ridiculous.

"The Ford Motor Company is known for letting really good products go stale," continued Christopher. "Toyota is the best at avoiding this trap. They always have something new coming out. They don't let a product get stale. They refresh it, they re-skin it, but they don't totally reengineer it like Ford does. Their process takes two to three years to refresh, compared to our four to six years. And what Ford ends up with in the end looks like a totally new vehicle. The Toyota refreshing process is a great example of using the correct engineering perspective. Their strategy is to refresh the product and keep it selling and keep tweaking it so that you can differentiate between model years. They have a continuous process of refreshing their products as opposed to the Ford Motor Company's process, which is based on totally reengineering the entire product every six to ten years. We reengineer the power train, the suspension, put in new technology, and reengineer it from one end to the other. Replacing the Escort and Taurus, which were great cars of premium quality, was crazy. They were the best in their class and number-one best sellers in their segments with a great value story."

"Why would anyone try to reinvent a product that was already selling so well?" Mr. Carman questioned.

"I certainly don't know!" replied Christopher.

It was a relief for Christopher to speak with someone who really listened and seemed to understand. He felt as if a huge weight had lifted off his shoulders. As he spoke, his heart felt lighter and he was hopeful, just having someone with whom he could share these concerns.

Mr. Carman turned to his friend.

"Tell me, my dear friend, what do you make of all this?" asked Mr. Carman.

The man leaned forward, took some more puffs from his cigar, and replied:

"In my days, my engineering team was persistent in their

efforts to design and produce a successful product that would be profitable, useful, reliable, cost-effective, and could improve the quality of people's lives. We could have made 8,495 different lightbulbs, but what if they all had ended up being defective? Would this invention have survived even to the twenty-first century as it has? Engineering without accountability and without an overall plan is irresponsible. We strived to make one excellent product that would outdo all others and stand the test of time. Products should also be strategically designed for compatibility and product evolution and be able to easily integrate into other platforms and systems.

"For example, our engineering team had developed a version of the lightbulb that was able to outstrip the other prototypes of inventors at the time, because of a combination of factors. We had an effective incandescent material, a higher vacuum than others were able to achieve, and a high-resistance lamp that made power distribution from a centralized source economically viable. Those factors made us successful in inventing an entire, integrated system of electric lighting.

"Let me share with you some lessons I've learned along the way. Remember that genius is 1 percent inspiration, and 99 percent perspiration. Also remember that just because something doesn't do what you planned it to do, it doesn't mean it's useless. And finally, remember that many of life's failures are people who did not realize how close they were to success when they gave up. And last but not least, be courageous! Whatever setback America has encountered, it has always emerged as a stronger and more prosperous nation."

"Thank you for sharing your experience and wisdoms with me. You can't imagine how helpful our conversation today has been. I can't believe you actually worked with the engineers that created one of the most important inventions in the history of the world—the lightbulb! You must have been very close to Mr. Edison?" said Christopher.

The man nodded.

"Sure was . . . heck of a guy!"

Mr. Carman and his friend chuckled.

Christopher had recalled seeing photos of Mr. Edison at the Henry Ford Museum only a few days ago, and this man's resemblance to Edison was remarkable. *Perhaps these old guys were so enamored by these great inventors that they actually emulated them in appearance and style,* thought Christopher. But even that rationalization didn't quite cut it, as it all seemed so real.

"Remember the speech you made to the crowd that cold rainy October night at the banquet hall?" Mr. Carman asked his friend.

'Yes, and I remember that my hands and voice were a bit shaky standing at the podium," replied his friend.

"You think you could remember some of it again? I'm sure Christopher would like to hear it," urged Mr. Carman.

The man thought for a moment and smiled.

"OK, it went something like this. . . . 'I would be embarrassed at the honors that are being heaped upon me this unforgettable night were it not for the fact that in honoring me, you are also honoring that vast army of thinkers and workers of the past. If I have helped spur men to greater effort, if our work has widened the horizon of thousands of men and given a measure of happiness in the world, I am content,'" the man recounted.

"And the last words of your speech were for me," said Mr. Carman proudly.

The man smiled.

"Yes, indeed. I believe I ended the speech with these final words: 'I can only say that in the fullest meaning of the term, he is my friend,'" said the man.

Christopher looked at the two men before him. It was a moment he would never forget and a message he would always remember. He looked across the fields far into the valley beyond. He felt proud to be a Ford man and to be an American. His thoughts drifted off into his own past. He remembered reciting his Boy Scout pledge, the Pledge of Allegiance to the Flag, and the Golden Rule. Christopher was thankful that such rituals had helped shape his life.

The sun stayed out until the three companions reached the main house. Then it began to rain. Christopher was lost in his thoughts for a few moments and didn't see Mr. Carman's friend leave. A melancholy mood had now moved in, and Mr. Carman seemed weary. His cough began to act up again.

"Tomorrow, same time, same place?" Christopher asked gently.

Mr. Carman nodded.

Albert suddenly arrived carrying a large heavy coat in his arms. He placed it over Mr. Carman's shoulders and walked him back to the Model T, where a driver was now waiting for them.

Mr. Carman turned to look back at the top of the hill and called out to Christopher, "And remember, **FORD** shouldn't stand for **F**ix **O**r **R**epair **D**aily,

FORD should stand for **F**ocusing **O**n **R**ealistic **D**esigns!"

CHAPTER SEVEN

Diversity Gone Wild!

It is all one to me if a man comes from Sing Sing Prison or Harvard. We hire a man—not his history. —Henry Ford

T he week was flying by, and there were only a few days left before the sixtieth anniversary of the death of Henry Ford. Christopher had spent the early part of the morning on the phone with Frank McIntyre, the reporter for the *Detroit Daily Herald*. The two had been discussing one of the most controversial subjects Frank was addressing in his article—diversity policies within the Ford Motor Company. Even though Frank was a trusted colleague, Christopher had still felt tense discussing the subject with him. He had been mindful to address the subject carefully. In fact, Frank had offered a few pointed questions that Christopher had requested they come back to later in the day. Christopher planned to have his meeting with Mr. Carman before tackling Frank's toughest questions. He had a feeling Mr. Carman could offer helpful insights into Ford's take on dealing with diversity and discrimination.

Christopher thought he would get to Fairlane Manor a little earlier than usual to prepare his thoughts. Heading down the hallway toward the elevator, he noticed his secretary, Jenny, walking toward him, holding a paper in her hand. Her expression was tense.

"I'm glad I caught you before you left. Wait 'til you read this!" she exclaimed. "It just came in over the wire."

Christopher glanced over the AP newswire and then looked up at Jenny who was anxiously waiting for his reaction to the news.

"Please give word that no one is to speak with any press—no emails, calls, nothing for now," Christopher directed. "Why don't you go ahead and schedule a department meeting with everyone this afternoon for three o'clock? I'll be back by then. And don't worry Jenny, everything will work out fine."

"Sure thing. Thanks, Mr. Hope," replied Jenny.

Christopher folded the newswire and put it in his jacket pocket. It was more bad news for the Ford Motor Company and more tough times ahead. He was so grateful to have Mr. Carman to turn to.

As it had since his first meeting with Mr. Carman, the weather always seemed to change as he approached Fairlane Manor. Clouds would suddenly appear and fog would begin to creep over the fields and highways. Christopher wasn't sure what to make of it, struggling to keep his focus on the task at hand and the incredible opportunity to speak with someone who had been there and seen it all. Mr. Carman, along with his friend's wise advice and his instinctive and uncanny ability to draw out from Christopher the unfiltered truth about what was really going on at Ford, was unique and remarkable. Mr. Carman was different from anyone Christopher had ever met before—a voice from the past with a vision for the future.

When Christopher pulled up to the gates of the manor, he could not believe his eyes. Crowds of elegantly dressed ladies wearing pearls, feathered hats, and furs, and gentlemen in formalwear, top hats, and spats were gathered around a parade of ten of the most beautiful antique Ford cars he had ever seen. They were laughing and walking around the cars, admiring them, sitting inside them, and chatting it up. Albert and a team of servants were moving about offering beverages and trays of snacks. There were also more plainly dressed folks wearing overalls, and Christopher guessed they were local farmers, workers, and car mechanics. He had never seen anything like it before. It was all unfolding like a dream in slow motion.

This must be a film, he thought to himself, but there were no cameras in sight. *Or maybe it's an auto collectors' club party.*

The parking attendant came running out to greet Christopher.

"Welcome, welcome, Mr. Hope!" said the attendant excitedly.

"What's happening here today?" Christopher asked.

"It's a parade of Mr. Carman's finest automobiles," the attendant exclaimed.

"Who are all these people?" asked Christopher. "Are they filming a movie or something?"

The attendant didn't have time to answer him. Mr. Carman was waving to him from the porch of the manor, motioning for Christopher to join him. As the attendant left to park his car, Christopher approached the crowd, excusing himself as he elbowed his way through. Before he got to the front porch, he stopped and admired the lineup of Mr. Carman's antique cars. They were all spectacular.

"Just in time for lunch, young man," said Mr. Carman when Christopher was within shouting distance.

"What is the occasion for the parade today?" Christopher inquired, hoping for a rational explanation.

"There's no occasion needed to spend a day admiring the work of American auto workers," replied Mr. Carman.

As they walked into the entrance of Fairlane Manor, Christopher turned around to take one last look at the crowd gathered on the front lawn. But when he did, he didn't know what to think. Everyone had instantly vanished. There was not one person in sight. All of the beautiful antique cars had disappeared too. It seemed impossible for everyone to have left so fast and for all the cars to have been driven away. There had been no sound of engines, only a light rain tapping.

Mr. Carman was already several paces ahead of him. As Christopher followed Mr. Carman up the steps toward the entrance, Fairlane Manor's timekeeper chimed seven times. Christopher counted each one as he walked toward the dining room. The fire was ablaze, and the lunch table was set for three people. Christopher wondered who their guest was today. He could see a man sitting at their table already waiting for them.

Albert offered to take Christopher's raincoat and led them into the dining hall.

"I've asked someone to join us for lunch. I believe that our topic today will be of great interest to him, and he may lend some insight to one of the most important issues facing the company and the nation," said Mr. Carman.

Christopher wondered if Mr. Carman had planned on discussing the issues of diversity today as well. It would be just like him to have known what was on Christopher's mind. Christopher took a closer look at the man seated at the table. He was a stout black man, impeccably dressed in a gray suit. His mustache was well trimmed and his fore brow indented with age lines. The man stood up to greet Christopher. He smiled warmly and offered his handshake to Christopher. The man had tremendous presence and magnetism.

As usual, Albert brought the cups of soybean tea and lunch began.

Christopher put his notepad on the table and then remembered the news release he had put in his pocket to show Mr. Carman.

"Well, before we start on our topic today, I have news to share with you," he announced to the group. "I just received this release from the Associated Press newswire."

Christopher took the press release from his jacket pocket and placed it on the table for the two men to see.

"The Ford Motor Company has fallen in ranks again and is now considered the fourth largest automobile company in the United States," recounted Christopher, visibly shaken by yet another major blow to the company. "Now, GM has taken the lead and ranked in first place, followed by Toyota in second, Daimler Chrysler in third, and then the Ford Motor Company in fourth place. For most of my career, Ford has been ranked second among the Big Three. Toyota passed us several months ago and now Daimler Chrysler has passed us to take the number-three slot. This is the first time in all my years with Ford that Daimler Chrysler has outsold us! Is this a sign of the times that Ford is no longer ranked among the Big Three? This is very bad news for Ford."

The three men sat quietly for a few moments. No one said a word. Each seemed reflective in his own thoughts.

Then Mr. Carman spoke.

"Well, Christopher, number four is better than number five," he said. Then, with a gleam in his eye, "What do you say we start plugging up the holes on the sinking ship and get it sailing once again? You know what they say—it ain't over 'til it's over! So, let's begin our topic of today and get on the

97

mend. We've got work to do and very little time to do it."

The other man at the table turned to Christopher and nodded encouragingly.

"Where does the Ford Motor Company stand today on diversity and the issue of discrimination, Christopher?" he beckoned. There was a glow about him, a spirituality of incredible power. Christopher felt safe and in the presence of greatness.

Christopher took a deep breath and cleared this throat.

"Sir, diversity has gone wild at the Ford Motor Company—absolutely wild!" began Christopher. "Diversity, in its purest form, is good and allows companies to leverage the opinions and experience of every employee. However, when diversity becomes an initiative or program, then corruption of the process can occur if not managed properly. It can sometimes create an environment where individual members of management can promote their own personal agendas under the umbrella of diversity. It has become a flagship issue for the Ford Motor Company over the years. It started as a noble effort, but quickly turned more into a quota program with numbers to be made. The initial noble effort was hijacked by people who used it to further their own interests instead of Ford's. Diversity programs have created a dissension and separation of employees. They have become a barrier to teamwork and a great source of inequality, rather than fairness, for the entire workplace."

"You know, it has always been my feeling that no value should be given to things beyond a person's control, such as gender, race, or ethnicity," Mr. Carman stated. "Such things do not guarantee success in business. Focusing on them devalues things that are controllable, like hard work, personal development, and the ability to deliver results. You know,

Henry Ford was the first to pay everyone the same wage for the same job, regardless of race, gender, or ethnicity. Fairness is an absolute practice for any business and, by definition, dictates equal treatment of all employees."

The guest raised his eyebrows at Mr. Carman's comment, and spoke up.

"My thoughts exactly!" said the man. "I dedicated my life to speaking out against practices of any kind that were based on ethnicity or race alone. True equality is a brotherhood that is colorblind, where race is not even an issue. We are all human, one and the same."

Christopher was taken aback by the man's statement. His words were so true, yet painted such a different picture of diversity than Ford's policies did.

"It's refreshing to hear such reasonable views on an issue that has become a distraction at Ford," said Christopher. "I agree that rather than worshiping diversity, through artificial programs, Ford should focus on celebrating the uniqueness of every employee. Everyone has uniqueness and can be valued for who they are and how they can contribute to the business. Not everyone is a member of a diverse group, but everyone is unique. Why not treat everyone the same?"

"Everyone *is* unique and everyone *should be* treated the same," exclaimed Mr. Carman. "Why don't you share with us some specific examples of Ford's diversity policies . . . gone wild?"

"Well, Ford's diversity policies began as a focus to hire more minority applicants," Christopher explained. "We were advised to pay a premium to hire minority applicants, regardless of their talent and experience in comparison to non-diverse applicants. This hiring quota policy extended to our promotion practices as well. Work group managers were forced to rank all minorities and move them above nondiverse performers. They were promised the fast track to management in Ford's oval offices. As minorities, many seemed to get an escalator to the top instead of having to take the stairs. They were not expected to obtain the prerequisite experience needed for success in top management roles because they were part of a protected class as minorities. Many just worked two or three years at Ford until a better offer surfaced outside of Ford. Their attitude was, 'I'm going to do what's best for me!' with little consideration for what was best for the company.

"In addition, compensation for minorities was not based on merit as it was for many other Ford employees. Ford's goal was to look good on paper or in the Ford Portrait to the world. Compensation, incentives, and bonuses for minorities became an entitlement program. As a result, Ford's business agenda was handicapped. Talented employees who could really help the business succeed were passed over by minority employees. At the same time, many very qualified minority employees who were already employed by the Ford Motor Company were passed over in favor of bringing in high-profile candidates from outside the company. It seemed that concerns with public perception and fanfare were prioritized ahead of putting the right person in the right job. As the diversity issue snowballed, minorities in leadership began to cater to their own agendas and sought to hire and promote other diverse employees. Their hiring decisions were not based on qualifications or performance, but again, rather, on ethnicity, race, or gender alone. These noncontrollable factors in hiring decisions created a reverse discrimination situation."

"That is why I always preached that discrimination of any kind is intolerable," said the man. "Unless you can find a way to be completely color blind when making decisions, true equality cannot be achieved."

"Equality was certainly not achieved through the diversity initiatives at Ford," said Christopher. "Once, many years ago, at a meeting of the top 100 Managers at the Ford Motor Company, the CEO at the time said in his address, 'I will strike you down if you don't hire and promote people of diversity over white males.' He then required every manager at Ford to view his speech. The result was that many talented proven performers did not perceive there to be a level playing field or a future at Ford and left our team.

"Then, Ford's diversity mantra worsened with the 'Diversity Is Our Strength' campaign. Ford tried to cram diversity down everyone's throats. Diversity became a tool used to promote certain leaders at the expense of a profitable business model. Ford got into a social agenda reform program, like the U.S. government, and became too fond of being politically correct. In the minds of Ford's leadership, diversity became the single most important ingredient that would ensure business profitability. There is no doubt that this was really one of the first steps toward the current situation wherein Ford had lost focus on obtaining a performance-driven workforce."

"Diversity of the workforce was always one of Ford's strengths," Mr. Carman interjected. "I think that the company falsely believes that if they make diversity a primary objective it will somehow guarantee or ensure the profitability of the business model. Well, it never has and never will. Diversity must not be prioritized at the expense of the business model. Diversity should be incorporated as a strength and part of the company's strategy, but not as a goal and certainly not as a guarantee to profitable success. Everyone brings something unique to the table, regardless of their race, ethnicity, or gender. Diversity should naturally be one of the strengths of every corporation."

"Yes," Christopher continued. "Ironically, Ford talks about increasing diversity in terms of minorities, women, and sexual orientation, but not in terms of diversity of opinions and perspectives. For example, Ford's view of diversity comes from a narrow geographic base," he explained. "In Ford's U.S. operations, approximately 75 percent of Ford employees come from Michigan or the area within one hundred miles of Detroit. The flip side of the coin is that less than 25 percent of Ford's vehicles are sold in that market. We primarily rely on Michigan-based universities and other systems within that narrow radius. That in itself represents an inbreeding of the same ideas at the expense of the company. If the Ford Motor Company were to truly embrace diversity, they would hire, promote, and retain more people from all over the United States. I believe that diversity should include having many perspectives represented, encouraging people to speak their minds, challenge the status quo, and push our company to be accountable to our shareholders and our customers. Diversity should not simply be about increasing the number of certain types of people."

"What about diversity with regard to age?" Mr. Carman questioned. "Does Ford have the sense to include a vast spectrum of ages into their ideas for diversity?"

"Unfortunately, the average age of Ford's workforce is getting younger all the time," Christopher answered. "There has been an unspoken quota for years to get rid of a large number of older employees. It's the old-white-guy syndrome that seems to support the idea that older white males are not a desirable part of the workforce. Ford leaders seem to disregard the fact that many of these older white employees have been among our top performers and loyal employees for many, many years. In fact, a former CEO launched a tier system that purposely disadvantaged older employees, regardless of their contribution. There were even statements made by a number of managers in meetings to the effect of 'This room will look a lot different in the future when some of you old white guys have to leave.' As you can imagine, such statements created a very hostile environment. Ford's diversity initiatives are chiefly focused on gender, racial, and ethnic diversity as its primary strategy for success, no matter what the cost to overall morale or the performance of the company."

"That is outrageous!" Mr. Carman barked. "It is the human capital that is the most important resource any business has. Ford cannot afford to lose any leaders, regardless of their diversity status."

"Diversity is an issue that also concerns the sexual orientation of employees," Christopher added. "Diversity at Ford definitely went wild in the company's decision to advertise in homosexual publications and begin catering to the homosexual agenda. In doing so, Ford became involved in driving a social agenda that did not relate in the least to profitability. In the United States, estimates show that less than 5 percent of the population is considered homosexual. It is estimated that less than 2 percent of Ford's current customers are homosexual. The Ford Motor Company's traditional values have always been mainstream and associated with family values. When we started championing the gay lifestyle, the American Family Association (AFA) came after us. They were outraged that we were advertising in gay publications and promoting gay sexuality. This launched a national controversy that contradicted our solid customer base of Americans who champion family values. The debate forced us to take a considerable portion of company resources away from focusing on the business model to deal with such a poor decision on advertising. Interestingly, however, the AFA did not go after the top six advertisers in gay publications, but only Ford, the seventh top advertiser in these publications. This is another example where some companies get a pass, but the American automobile companies are singled out. A full-fledged boycott followed the AFA's outrage with Ford. Some of our senior managers, in coordination with key dealers, met with the American Family Association (AFA). They made an agreement that when our advertising contracts ran out, they would not be renewed. As soon as they had made this deal, the AFA backed off of their protests and boycotts. There are simply some issues in which Ford as a company should stay out of."

"Ford customers have historically been average, hardworking Americans," said Mr. Carman. "If the majority of Ford customers represent one side of an issue, the company shouldn't be involved in promoting the other side so blatantly. Ford must be loyal to its customers."

"Ford's dealers definitely felt the same way you do," said Christopher. "As a result of the widely publicized reaction of the American Family Association to our advertising in gay publications, our dealer network went crazy. They were getting complaints from irate customers who could not believe the family-values company they had supported for years would do that. We put our dealers and managers at risk by putting them in the middle of a highly controversial social issue. We put them in the position of having to handle numerous irate phone calls from customers. Meanwhile, Ford did nothing but give arrogant and ridiculous responses. Like ostriches, they put their heads in the sand and hoped the problems would just go away.

"The type of message Ford was sending by advertising in certain publications started at the top of our company with some of the management being very liberal and trying to drive a liberal agenda," Christopher explained. "In fact, some of the guys at the top who wanted to continue to promote their social agenda decided to reverse the agreement with the AFA. They went right back to placing controversial advertising again.

"There is little doubt in my mind that this misguided approach to diversity was one of the first steps in the recent erosion of our business," Christopher declared. "Driving out personal agendas on company time and with company money caused us to lose focus on having a performance-driven workforce. Instead of top performers being promoted accordingly, this so-called diversity agenda began dictating who got promotions and so forth. As Ford began to lose in profitability due in part to their biased hiring and promotion practices, the luxury of looking the other way and not focusing on key skill sets of employees or prospective employees could no longer be afforded."

"Incredible!" exclaimed Mr. Carman. "Every company in America and in the world could relate to this."

"Absolutely!" Christopher agreed. "It is a serious case of political correctness gone amok. Ford was not a noninclusive work environment in the first place. We treated everyone with respect in our workplace. The fact that we never had a lot of discrimination suits supports our history of inclusiveness. Everyone in the company would agree that we need to continue to create and sustain a work environment that allows every employee to be productive without harassment, regardless of race, gender, or ethnicity. Such a work environment has always existed at Ford, and it still does today."

"Ford shouldn't be driving social agendas at all!" Mr. Carman exclaimed. "Ford's agenda should be focused on running a profitable company, and they should steer away from social agendas."

"I agree," said Christopher. "Our company does our best work when we stay away from social agendas and focus on the business model and on the market ahead.

"The ability in recent years of some of our top leaders to waste millions of company dollars on their personal agendas is not only limited to diversity issues," Christopher added. "For instance, a significant percentage of our customers are NASCAR fans. But, in the past, some Ford managers preferred Formula One racing and poured millions of dollars into Formula One racing. At the same time, they kept racing legends and others on the Ford payroll to advise us about Formula One racing. There was no accountability for the negative impact this had on company profitability. Our Formula One racing investment should represent a very small part of Ford's budget in relation to NASCAR, because our customer demographics lean closer to NASCAR than they do Formula One racing."

"That just sounds like common sense to me," Mr. Carman retorted.

"One thing that doesn't relate to common sense at all is the fact that, in the name of diversity, the Ford Company has segmented our employees into what are called Employee Resource Groups," Christopher fired back. "These support groups, in fact, create a barrier to unity. Some of these employee groups include: the Ford-employee African

American Network (FAAN), the Ford Asian Indian Association (FAIA), the Ford Chinese Association (FCA), the Ford Finance Network (FFN), the Ford Gay, Lesbian or Bisexual Employees (GLOBE), the Ford Hispanic Network Group (FHNG), the Professional Women's Network (PWN), the Women in Finance (WIF), the Ford Parenting Network (FPN), the Ford Interfaith Network (FIN), the Middle Eastern Community @ Ford Motor Company, and the Ford Employees Dealing with DisAbilities (FEDA). I might have missed a few, but that's a good number of them," said Christopher.

"It makes me dizzy just trying to remember them all," said Mr. Carman, shaking his head.

"Tell me about it!" said Christopher. "It's a wonder anyone can keep them all straight. I'm not saying that there is anything wrong with having support groups within the company, but we cannot take them to the extent that Ford has. These separate groups do more to promote individuality than unity. They force us all to focus on the differences we have rather than what we have in common. We should treat everyone equally instead of taking sides."

"Absolutely!" concurred Mr. Carman. "Finding support from those who share common experiences with you is one thing. Promotion of social agendas does not belong in the workplace."

"One manager in particular was the driving force behind the Ford African American Network (FAAN). Ford hired him after acquiring his company as a part of an acquisition deal. Because he was an African American man, Ford leaders also saw this as a quick way to put a minority in a top leadership role and placed him in charge of the Ford Customer Service Division (FCSD) as a senior manager. Unfortunately, this man had very little knowledge about customer service or FCSD. In the first two years, he insisted on restructuring the division, which cost the company millions in revenues, stripping away focus from our revenue-generating programs. He brought several nonqualified managers into FCSD based on the FAAN's agenda. It quickly became evident that these managers had been appointed based on their race and gender, which created a very difficult environment for our employees to work in. This manager, during his tenure, cost the company astronomical amounts.

"Also, this same manager was always traveling on the weekends to many of our regional offices and borrowing company cars for personal use, then leaving them parked at airports in short-term parking with absolutely no idea where he had left them. Once in Philadelphia, he left a car parked in two feet of snow for over a month before our people at Ford were able to locate it. We had to pay quite a hefty parking bill for that blunder. This occurred over half a dozen times. He just didn't seem to care that the regional offices would have to immobilize two people for two days to search for where he had left our cars, and he would not even apologize."

Mr. Carman rolled his eyes.

The man next to him exclaimed: "I don't know whether to laugh or cry. I can't believe what I'm hearing. This is absolutely an abuse of diversity policy!"

"Well, I still haven't told you about our Dealer Development program," added Christopher with a sigh. "Originally, Ford's Dealer Development program was designed to bring in new dealers—people who had the right skill sets and understood the business, but lacked the resources to start a dealership on their own. Through the Dealer Development program, Ford offered to give these potential dealers financial help and training to get started. Ford would continue supporting them until they were up and running and able to buy the dealership. The intent was to develop the strength of our dealer network. It was really a great program which allowed many young up-and-coming dealership employees to come in and get a start with Ford's support.

"Unfortunately, it didn't take long for the Dealer Development Program to turn into a quota-driven program. It became a feel-good deal where Ford mainly sought out minorities for the program. Many of the dealers recruited during the quota-driven era of the Dealer Development program ended up being some of our least loyal dealers and—not to mention—the least profitable. But, nonetheless, Ford was able to hold its picture-perfect diverse head high saying, 'Hey, look how many minority dealers we have and that we support!' Once again, well-intentioned efforts had fallen prey to social agendas. The Dealer Development program was, in fact, a great program for any dealer needing assistance whether they were a minority or not. Instead, many potentially great dealers miss out on the opportunity and the program struggles from a profitability standpoint because of Ford's intense focus on diversity being the ultimate priority."

"But you are running a business that's based on profitability—capitalism at its finest—not on a social agenda!" interrupted Mr. Carman, markedly agitated. "It's a crying shame that such a program overlooked many qualified potential Ford dealers."

"The Dealer Development program costs the company millions each year," Christopher added. "Under this program, not only did Ford recruit minority dealership owners as a rule, but they often replaced a local, experienced dealer with a minority dealership owner who had little or no retail dealership experience. Ford also recruited minority dealership owners from other companies, again discounting local expertise. The minority dealers were provided intense training programs to try to make up for their lack of experience, and this remedial program additionally cost the company hundreds of thousands of dollars. During this program, some of the dealers' inability to perform was magnified. Many of them failed during the first three years. After an incredible company expense to train them with little or no accountability for results, many of them surrounded themselves with family members and friends who also lacked the skills to be successful in the automobile business.

"Believe it or not, we actually had a mandate that no new dealers would be added anywhere in the country until the minority dealership quota was met. Our primary focus was on African Americans, and later we turned to women minorities and Hispanics. We also ignored geographical considerations. I can remember one instance when we put a Dealer Development program store with a black man in Alabama. If you looked in the city's telephone book, there is a phone number for the Knights of the Ku Klux Klan less than four blocks from where the dealership was located. The probability of this dealership's success was compromised by the strange environment where we put it. We set the dealer up for failure," said Christopher, shaking his head.

"That's moronic!" exclaimed Mr. Carman.

"How destructive!" the man exclaimed.

"Once again, they neglected to look at the reality of the situation," continued Christopher. "Some of the candidates they had placed into this program lacked capital and experience in working in automobile dealerships. This program lost money because they didn't have the accountability and their expense structure was out of whack. It was not managed properly and had become a huge write-off. We should focus instead on performance-driven candidates in this dealer startup program. If it were based on that, then it would be a tremendous program."

Mr. Carman shook his head, stunned by Christopher's recounting. Then he cracked a little smile, breaking the intensity of the conversation.

"Sounds like the lights are on but nobody's home!" he laughed. "Well, as Will Rogers used to say: 'You know everybody is ignorant, only on different subjects.'"

The third man politely smiled. He was listening with quiet intent, hands folded on his chest, and Christopher could sense tension building. He hesitated in continuing further, but Mr. Carman nudged him on.

"Please continue, Christopher," he encouraged.

"The Ford Motor Company has provided the dealers with funding and given them the opportunity to succeed as automobile dealers with very little accountability," Christopher went on. "The Ford Motor Company likes the idea of the Dealer Development program even though it has very poor business results because the program has been managed irresponsibly. Even with all that Ford gives to many of the Dealer Development program dealers, when they have the opportunity to use discretionary Ford products, many of these dealers lack loyalty to Ford and consistently choose to use non-Ford products such as financing, extended warranties, bulk oil, accessories, et cetera.

"The core business model must focus on experience, knowledge of the business, and a track record of success along with a history of demonstrating the ability to get the job done. When Dealer Development dealers were put in, some of our best minority employees were overlooked. We had strong minority candidates inside the Ford Motor Company who should have been given the opportunity to go retail. It's like legal immigration versus illegal immigration, where people go through a certain process of immigration and then they emerge as good citizens. Companies should have the same process where people go through the companies and as they are trained and understand the environment, they become more productive employees. Within a big corporation, and this isn't just Ford, when you have someone who has not done the right things, has not followed the rules nor earned their stripes, and they jump ahead of someone else who has done those things, solely because of diversity, it is just like amnesty to the illegal immigrant, and it sends the wrong message.

"And that's what we've done with diversity. We've sent the wrong message to good employees. The message has been that all that matters is your gender, race, or ethnicity. Even our top-performing employees are made to feel that someone else is going to jump ahead of them, just because of their race or gender. Such feelings of insecurity bring lots of problems. This fosters an environment of inequality. That's precisely what has happened at the Ford Motor Company with diversity gone wild!

"It is risky when a company decides to hire, promote, or put in a place of power an employee or business partner based only on their God-given gender, race, or ethnicity. Performance and skill sets of employees should trump gender, race, and ethnicity," concluded Christopher. He sat back in his chair and took a sip of tea.

All of a sudden, the man who had been sitting next to Christopher listening quietly pounded his fist on the table, shattering the silence like an earthquake in a glass factory. His powerful voice reverberated throughout the manor.

"They got it all wrong! They have taken what I said and scandalized it! They completely misunderstood what I was trying to tell them! I shared my dream with them, my dream which they quote over and over again—that one day, every valley shall be exalted, every hill and mountain shall be made low, the rough places will be made plain, and the crooked places will be made straight, and the glory of the Lord shall be revealed, and all flesh shall see it together. Not blacks, or whites, or segmented minorities but all people under one God. ALL people! I will not rest until I am certain beyond all doubt that they understood," continued the man with a trembling force. His voice echoed throughout Fairlane Manor and out the door into the valley, over the hills and through the inner cities, and everywhere. And Christopher hoped his voice could also be heard echoing throughout the offices of management at Ford's world headquarters.

The man continued, "I said that in spite of the difficulties and frustrations of the moment, I still have a dream. It is a dream deeply rooted in the American Dream and that one day this nation will rise up and live out the true meaning of its creed—We hold these truths to be self-evident—that all men are created equal. Equality must not be a weapon used to discriminate. Doing so is a crime against humanity and a grave sin in the eyes of God.

"Christopher, you must go back and tell them again what I said, because I will not rest until they get it right, until they understand. Remind them again, and again, that when we let freedom ring, when we let it ring from every village and every hamlet, from every state and every city, we will be able to speed up that day when all of God's children, black men and white men, Jews and Gentiles, Protestants and Catholics, will be able to join hands and sing in the words of the old Negro spiritual, 'Free at last! Free at last! Thank God Almighty, we are free at last!' Remind them over and over until they truly understand."

Christopher lowered his eyes, and when he looked up, the man was gone. Christopher placed his elbows on the table and put his head in his hands. He closed his eyes. *Am I imagining all of this, or was this magnificent man really who my heart tells me he was? What's going on with me? Is the dream inside me so strong that I can will all this to happen? Maybe as Shakespeare said, the world* is *a stage and we are* all *actors. And if it is, I have been entrusted with a major role and a great responsibility.*

Mr. Carman began to cough spasmodically and held on to the chair railing for strength to stand up. Christopher had seen Mr. Carman's health weaken as the days passed.

"Christopher, Ford's diversity program seems to have started off as a good initiative but became misguided. They have made a tactical error by ignoring the traditional values of their customers, employees, and dealers in this new-style marketing strategy. That is why the program has failed. Remember that you cannot be all things to all people and cater to the minority at the expense of the majority. That's just bad business," concluded Mr. Carman.

Albert brought Christopher his raincoat from the cloak-room.

It was time to go.

"I'll see you tomorrow, same time, same place," Mr.

Carman told Christopher, as he waved good-bye, "and remember,

FORD should stand for **F**ocusing **O**n **R**esponsible **D**iversity!"

CHAPTER SIX

The Compensation Collapse

The man who will use his skill and constructive imagination to see how much he can give for a dollar, instead of how little he can give for a dollar, is bound to succeed.

—Henry Ford

The weather was unusually cold for a spring day. When Christopher arrived at Fairlane Manor, the winds had picked up and the fog in front of the house was so dense you could barely see its form, except for the white smoke circling out of the chimney. Today seemed different from all the others. Albert had been waiting to greet him at the front entrance.

"You and Mr. Carman will be dining alone, Mr. Hope. Mr. Carman wasn't up for any visitors. He was quite busy this morning working on the electrical generator. He had only wanted to lunch with you today," explained Albert.

"What seems to be the problem with the generator? Can I give him a hand?" asked Christopher.

"Oh no, sir, no need. It will all work out. But thank you kindly," replied Albert.

As the days passed by, Christopher was regaining a sense of confidence and value. He was comfortable at Fairlane Manor. It felt almost like home to him, different from the modernized Fairlane Manor he had known before meeting Mr. Carman.

He knew his way to the cloakroom and hung up his raincoat right next to Mr. Carman's. Christopher glanced up at the old grandfather clock and noticed that the hour hand was still halted at seven on the nose. And then the clock began to chime seven times. Christopher counted each one as he walked with Albert into the dining hall where Mr. Carman had been waiting for him.

Christopher had begun to develop a taste and liking for soybeans. He found them to have soothing and healing qualities. He sipped his tea slowly, more aware of his surroundings than before. The fire intensified and cast shadows on the walls. The lights flickered on and off, and he thought he had heard music playing, the old kind of melodies like the AM radio played in his car when Mr. Carman rescued him on the highway. It was coming from a room somewhere down the long dark hallway. The humming noise he had once heard before, which sounded like a generator of sort, was louder today. *That's probably the generator Mr. Carman was working on this morning*, thought Christopher. He took his notebook and pen from his jacket pocket and placed it on the table. He began to share his grief with Mr. Carman about his colleague and friend, John, who had been given an early retirement package, and then launched into his view of the failures in the compensation system at the Ford Motor Company. Mr. Carman listened compassionately, again troubled by what Christopher was sharing with him and bothered by what seemed to be a cough that just wouldn't quit.

"Compensation must be tied to tangible results and performance measures. There must be accountability," stated Christopher. "Rainmakers—those producing results—must be identified and developed. At the same time, calculated risk-taking and accountability must be woven into the environment and must replace the current don't-rock-the-boat strategy. We need results-oriented managers with a sense of passion for the business. We need managers focused on doing the right things rather than politically correct managers who spend more time working on getting their next job than doing their current one. Some of our current managers seem to spend more time trying to look like things are right than doing the right things. There needs to be an overhaul of the compensation system and other rewards and incentives to tie them to positive business results rather than political correctness."

"In my experience," Mr. Carman explained, "managers must be servant leaders with a long-term view and allegiance to the people. If they are primarily in it for the money, they will never be successful long-term."

"You're absolutely right. At Ford, compensation for many of the employees is no longer based on performance or achieving business results, and the promotion system motivates the wrong kinds of behavior and causes us to lose many of our top performers.

"Let me explain how Ford's compensation system works. It used to function well, and then things shifted in the early 1980s. Compensation, or what we call the pay plan, was based on achieving specific targets and business results. Managers were graded on how their dealers performed in their zone—not just for their management style. Division managers were paid based on how their division performed. However, senior management had resented this because they thought that the company's results were based on their own great management abilities and that these results had nothing to do with the employees' performance. Therefore, they developed an idea which they called 'merit planning.' It sounded good and was originally a well-intentioned process. However, it ended up being administered more like an entitlement program as managers handed out similar pay raises to almost everyone, paying little attention to performance. The spread between the top performers' compensation and the lowest performers became less than 3 percent. The spread was unrealistic for the variance in employee contributions. The company couldn't put their money where the production was—to reward those who were really performing. So everyone got a watered-down merit plan, except for senior managers who grabbed with both hands more than they had deserved. Employees did not perceive a relationship between their performance and their compensation. They described this merit plan as a great improvement and told us that we would be more motivated and successful, but it was like putting perfume on a pig—it still smelled badly and nobody bought it!"

"What happened to the middle guys, the ones who actually generate revenues?" Mr. Carman asked.

"The top managers got more than they should have," answered Christopher. "Then, because of our posturing with the UAW and our unwillingness to have them be angry with us as they often were at GM, the UAW took more than they should have. The result was the middle managers—those who were actually working with the dealers and customers and achieving results—got crunched. There is only 100 percent of a dollar, and no one at either end was willing to give up their percentage. The focus shifted to the elite management and put the compensation in the hands of those furthest from the customer," he explained.

"The promotion system is even more complex and bizarre. Ford, as several large companies used to have, has a system called right-of-assignment. This means that in order to go up to the next grade level, you may have to relocate to another part of the country and often simply at the behest of some misguided regional manager. Or worse, when an insecure manager viewed you as an up-and-coming leader, they might ship you out for no business reason to protect their empire so you were not a threat by outperforming them. Most of the time, these opportunities to excel were classified as developmental or lateral moves, not promotions, so you were not actually getting a promotion in terms of job responsibilities. If you were not willing to relocate, you were not considered loyal or top management material, despite your performance metrics. Each relocation cost the company an average of $50,000 to $250,000 in relocation expenses and incentives. In order to move up in the company, in many instances, you had to move to a new geographic location, even on a lateral basis in title or responsibility. In addition, to move up, you also have to serve time in Detroit.

"As a result, we have had many demoralized employees who had to leave their community where they were performing at a high level to start all over in another part of the country. This really placed tremendous stress on the home life, particularly since today there are more and more two-career couples. The company would rationalize that it valued the employee's family and personal life and then at the same time expect the employee to uproot their family every few years. Talk about not encouraging diversity, especially of women employees whose husbands worked, expecting that the working spouses of our employees—male or female—should sacrifice their jobs every few years so Ford can relocate their spouse. We lost some of our best future leaders who were unwilling to stay with the company with this archaic approach of moving around to move up.

"It seemed that many of the relocations were just to have some experience pass-through and get a box checked on your employee profile. In quite a number of cases, when the person was relocated, they did not have the right skill sets for the job and they were unable to perform, leaving the other employees in that location to fill in for the new person who could not do it. This caused tensions for those doing the new person's job for them and made them more resentful of the new person joining that location. This was a lose-lose situation.

"The other side of the coin was that because so many employees did not want to move from the location they loved, they would not perform at top levels because they feared if they did too good of a job they would be promoted and have to relocate their family. So Ford lost great people who left the company to keep from having to move and lost performance from others who did not want to leave Ford but did not want to have to move if they excelled and then were targeted to move up. If you added the disincentive of relocation if you excelled to the small difference in compensation between an average performance and an outstanding one—roughly 3 percent of your compensation, why would anyone want to contribute their best? This has created a lowest-common-denominator mind-set when we should have been creating leaders at all levels and in all locations since few, if any, companies have too many leaders," said Christopher.

"Another problem with the incentives and lack of accountability is in our marketing relationships. We have had hot-shot marketing leaders in the company come in, only planning to stay for a short time. They overpay our vendors for marketing services in order to build a relationship with them so they can go to work there when they leave Ford. No one is watching the store and holding them accountable. As soon as they are held accountable or asked to produce, they bolt like gold miners going to a new mine. Then, surprise, surprise! They end up in jobs at some of our major vendors they were overpaying with Ford's money."

"So this right-of-assignment rule and your overall promotion system seem crazy, especially in order to attract the young people of today. It also seems that it would have a negative impact on the employees developing long-term relationships with the dealers in their markets. The company should value employees that produce great results, while fostering relationships with the dealers, customers, and their communities," said Mr. Carman.

"For some strange reason, the company seems to fear the dealer relationship—can't get too close," explained Christopher.

"That's complete nonsense!" quipped Mr. Carman. "How can you have good dealer partners without a relationship built on trust, integrity, and consistency?"

"You're so wise, Mr. Carman. We should be encouraging and rewarding our employees who thrive with their dealer partners. Without successful dealers, how do we sell and service our cars and trucks?" asked Christopher.

"It seems that the company's management has confused activity with accomplishment. I always said that a rocking chair has activity, but it's not going anywhere," said Mr. Carman.

"Exactly! And just think of the great employees we could have retained and the millions of dollars wasted on unnecessary relocation expenses!" explained Christopher.

"There is no two ways about it. Compensation must be tied to performance," injected Mr. Carman. "That's the bottom line."

"An effective, but short-lived, example of tying rewards to performance was a program the company launched called the 'Continuous Improvement Recognition Program.' It saved Ford a ton of money," continued Christopher.

"And what is that?" asked Mr. Carman.

"Any employee could present an idea to improve efficiency or save costs. It got every employee engaged in trying to cut costs and improve results. Many great ideas and actions were submitted. The program cost Ford about a million a year in compensation to those who submitted ideas and it saved Ford hundreds of millions of dollars. But they ended up cutting the program because they thought the company was paying too much money to the mid-manager and nonmanager levels, and top managers didn't qualify for this program," explained Christopher.

Mr. Carman shook his head.

"What? Are you telling me that the company cut a program which cost only one million a year but saved them hundreds of millions of dollars? Can't they count? On top of that, it empowered employees and engaged them more fully in the business. Are they crazy? Have they forgotten the purpose of it all?" exclaimed Mr. Carman, his voice cracking. He removed his handkerchief from his vest pocket and held it up to his mouth. He began to cough, having a hard time catching his breath.

Christopher paused and waited for Mr. Carman to regain his composure.

Albert suddenly entered the dining hall with a handful of fire logs and placed them into the fire, where the flames had begun to dwindle.

"We'll get this fire going, sir, and it will be much warmer in here in a few minutes."

"Thanks, Albert," replied Mr. Carman, as his cough began to subside.

The new firewood began to catch on and crackle and the room warmed up nicely.

They resumed their conversation.

"Ford's compensation program is in fact an overcompensation program that pays out millions of dollars to the CEO and top managers. This money is basically stolen from the middle managers. The general salary rule is Robin Hood in reverse: steal from the poor to give to the rich. As was reported by a local news source, Ford's president of the Americas spends in the ball park of seventy thousand dollars a week for flights from his home to work; receives a $1 million bonus; receives three hundred thousand dollars of non-related company work expenses; gets high-flying perks, et cetera. Some of our top management have been living in La La Land and have been behaving more like celebrity rock stars and pro athletes rather than responsible business managers. All of this is occurring while we are reporting record losses and laying off thousands of workers because of a lack of money. Unfortunately, many of the Ford leaders have become self-serving, short-term thinkers with a keen and constant eye on lining their own pockets. There has been a shift from pay for performance to pay for perceived ability to perform and pay for diversity and no accountability for results," continued Christopher.

Mr. Carman was exasperated.

"This compensation and promotion model will wear you down. They are tossing their employees overboard!" exclaimed Mr. Carman. "Now, what about the dealers—how do they fare with all of Ford's decisions?"

"Ford recently announced to the dealerships that they are going to have a reduced market share. They are gearing down to a combined car and truck share goal of 14 to 15 percent of the U.S. market. That's down from 22 percent. Our dealers are being forced to restructure so they can still be profitable with this reduction in sales. Many will be forced to take on another franchise to offset the lost revenue, and others will go out of business. Without profitable dealers, we will never reach our sales goals. Top management seems to forget that fact and behave as if the dealers are unimportant or that they owe us their livelihood. Yes, the Ford Motor Company allows them to have their franchise, but historically we have made tons of money off their hard work, and we would not exist as a company today without them. Look at the other major manufacturers—do any of them exist without distributors or dealers? This current situation is really very tough on our dealers. Their facilities were constructed based on a 20-plus percent market share. They are very anxious, and many of them believe that the Ford Motor Company has sold out on them, by not representing their best interests at this time. Some of our long-standing and loyal Ford dealers are going to be out of business."

"Ford needs to provide incentives to all levels of the company for progress toward goals and objectives, and not just for profits," Mr. Carman explained. "Ford needs to reward top performers and leaders with not only a fair share of the compensation pie, but also with recognition for all they do, instead of letting people above them take all the credit. If you do this, perhaps you can stop the mass exodus of talented people leaving because they perceive they are not valued. The company must also spend time and energy trying to communicate more effectively with their employees and dealers as you work through this uncomfortable time period."

"This transformation will be very difficult, Mr. Carman, but we cannot let it be the beginning of the end," said Christopher. "However, a recent employee survey in North America revealed that less than 50 percent of the Ford employees believed the Way Forward plan would help Ford achieve a sustainable business success. Only 34 percent believed we had the right product line, and only 47 percent have confidence in the company's long-term success. Many of those surveyed were long-term employees who have always been very optimistic about our future in past surveys.

It's important and fair to note that this survey was taken during the exact time Ford was undertaking a reorganization of the entire company. We desperately need a strategic plan that our employees and dealers believe in and will rally around."

"Keep a good record of these notes, Christopher, and everything you are sharing with me. They will be very useful and important in the coming day's ahead," said Mr. Carman. "I've got some work to do on the generator today, and not a lot of time to fix it."

"Sure I couldn't take a look at it with you? I'm really pretty handy with motors and electricity. I'm sort of a hands-on kind of guy," smiled Christopher.

Mr. Carman laughed.

"Thanks again, Christopher. That's mighty thoughtful of you but I think that the Ford *Motor* Company needs some fixing too, so you go head back to headquarters—they really need you there. And don't worry about me—I'll be on my way real soon."

A cold wind blew through the dining hall and the lights flickered.

It was time to go. They walked side by side to the entrance. Christopher fetched his raincoat from the cloakroom.

"I'll see you tomorrow then, same time, same place," Mr. Carman said to Christopher, as he waved goodbye to him from the front porch. And remember,

FORD should stand for **F**ocusing **O**n **R**ewarding **D**eliverables!"

CHAPTER FIVE

The Union—Rearranging the Seats on the Titanic

You will find men who want to be carried on the shoulders of others, who think that the world owes them a living. They don't seem to see that we must all lift together and pull together. —Henry Ford

C hristopher planned to talk with Mr. Carman about the union at their lunch appointment later that day. As he was preparing for their meeting, he began to think about the thousands of dedicated and proud Ford and UAW workers he came to know over the years. He remembered the diehard loyalty and the spirit that most of them possessed. In fact, Christopher truly believed that if most of them were cut, they would bleed Ford blue. He wondered what would become of all the friends that he had made in the factories, plants, and parts depots.

On several of his many assignments while moving up through Ford, Christopher had the privilege of having his office located on site at the plants and depots alongside UAW workers. He found that the vast majority of the employees were good, loyal, and proud people who had unknowingly been working under a bad contract. Christopher knew that if these contracts were not altered, they could surely kill the golden goose of the Ford Motor

Company. Many jobs were at stake.

Many of Christopher's friends would, from time to time, share with him that they knew the union deal was bad for Ford Motor Company in that it favored the union too much. But his friends also knew that pointing out any union-friendly flaws in a union meeting would be the same as taking your life into your hands. As a result, most union employees had chosen to ride this bus for as long as they could.

Christopher had heard many stories from his friends about the crazy things that some of their UAW co-workers would do. Most of the funny stories were innocuous incidents such as an employee simply not coming to work after a ball game or long weekends. Some of the stories centered on employees who just tended to hang out during the work day without focus—and without doing their job. Inevitably, these stories were always concluded by Christopher's friends saying something like, "And you know what frustrates the Ford managers the most is that they can't enforce good work behaviors because of the current UAW contract which protects even those who don't work!"

Working for Ford seemed like a game to a small percentage of employees who felt they had a license to do whatever they could to frustrate management without any repercussions.

Christopher knew that there was a time when unions were needed to protect the rights and safety of employees. In recent years, however, the focus had shifted from protection to holding companies hostage for higher pay for less work, more benefits, and less accountability—all at a cost to the United States of declining competitiveness versus foreign products.

As Christopher was sifting and sorting though his

thoughts, the telephone rang, reminding him that he had a busy day ahead of him.

"Christopher here," he answered.

"Good morning, Mr. Hope. It's Albert. I'm calling to ask you if it wouldn't be an imposition to come to Fairlane Manor for tea this afternoon, rather than lunch. Mr. Carman has invited a special guest, and unfortunately she will not be able to make it in time for lunch."

"I think anytime this afternoon would be fine," replied Christopher, as he quickly clicked open his calendar on his laptop. "This afternoon would be great. I can move my schedule up and work straight through lunch. That will free me up to leave earlier today. What time would be convenient for Mr. Carman and his guest?"

"Shall we say four o'clock then?" confirmed Albert.

"Sure thing!" said Christopher.

"Mr. Carman will be expecting you," said Albert.

She? thought Christopher. *Who could she be*, he wondered with a playful curiosity, because he had only remembered seeing men around the manor on most of his visits.

The afternoon had flown by. He had glanced at his watch, and four o'clock was rapidly approaching. The sun was lowering in the sky. It was time to leave for his meeting at Fairlane Manor. He took his raincoat off the coat hook and walked toward the elevators. As he drove out of the parking garage into the busy Dearborn traffic, he noticed a street vendor at the corner selling flowers. He thought that perhaps he should bring something for Mr. Carman's guest. Christopher bought a small bouquet of red roses.

The weather began to change once again as it had all the days before on his way to Fairlane Manor. And in no time, he was there, driving up to the front gates. The parking attendant came out as usual to park his car, and Albert arrived at the top of the stairs to greet him.

Once inside, he handed his coat to Albert and walked down the hallway toward the dining room. The old grandfather clock chimed its melancholy notes.

The table was set for tea, with fine china and trays of scones, cookies, tea sandwiches, jams, and a large pot of soybean tea. Seated at the table were Mr. Carman and a sophisticated and stately looking woman. A fur shawl was wrapped around her shoulders. A strand of large white pearls adorned her elegant black dress of an older-style fashion. Her wide-brimmed, oval-shaped felt hat was cocked to the side of her head and decorated with an elaborately bejeweled pin. The lady had a handsomely striking face with penetrating dark and kind eyes and a great big smile. There was an aurora of light radiating from her presence.

Christopher offered the lady the bouquet of red roses he had brought especially for her.

"Oh, how thoughtful! My husband and I have nurtured a rose garden for many years at our estate at Hyde Park. I've kept a close watch on them, you know, as they require constant care," said the lady, placing the rose bouquet on her lap.

Christopher sat down, took his pen and paper out of his pocket, and glanced up again to catch another quick look at the stately figure seated at his side. There was no question in his mind as to who she was. And who could he tell? Who would believe him? Was it important anyway? *If it was a dream, delusion, vision, reality, or his perception of reality, did it really matter?* Christopher reflected. He was the ultimate spin doctor who lived in a world where reality was about perception and dictated by those who had the power and the money. With each meeting with Mr. Carman, Christopher's journey for the truth took on more significance and meaning than he could have ever anticipated. This was about more than writing press stories and the opportunity to vent years of frustrations. His search had led him on a gut-wrenching and challenging path.

"Well, as we had planned, I'd like to share with you the state of things at the Ford Motor Company today, regarding our relationship with the United Auto Workers," said Christopher, his voice somewhat hesitant as a shyness came over him.

Somehow instinctively, Mr. Carman always knew how to break the ice and make everyone relaxed, especially Christopher.

"You know what Will Rogers once said?" said Mr. Carman with a silly grin: "Live in such a way that you would not be ashamed to sell your parrot to the town gossip."

Everyone laughed, and then the lady turned to Christopher and said, "So, tell me Mr. Hope, about the state of affairs of the company and our nation today in relation to the union and human rights. Although I have many years of experience in this regard, the world has changed quite a bit, and I would like to learn more about where we have hopefully evolved," said the lady.

"Madam, it's my honor, and I hope I will not be offensive in my attempt to be honest and frank," explained Christopher. "There are many challenges facing the Ford Motor Company regarding the union and human rights. The economic deals that we have cut with the union are financial suicide. There is the lack of strong commitment and relationship between the union and the Ford Motor Company. There is the lack of motivation on behalf of the union workers for individual or company performance.

"Our present contract and relationship with the UAW is a set-up for failure," Christopher continued. "I believe deep down that most UAW employees would agree. Heck, their membership has declined from 1.5 million in 1979 to 576,000 in 2006. They are tired of typical manufacturing where you come in, put in your time, and go home. Yet we continue to operate with a shirts-versus-skins mentality, and by that I mean management versus labor—a completely archaic system of operation."

Christopher added, "Our current labor costs are way out of line when compared to other players in the Big Six—the three major American companies and Toyota, Honda, and Nissan. It just so happens that Toyota, Honda, and Nissan are nonunion. The current arrangements with the unions in the United States have driven jobs out of the States, and it keeps us from being competitive in a super-competitive industry. We should strive to align hourly wages more closely with the prevailing manufacturing pay in the states where each plant is located. That is what Toyota is trying to do in setting their wage standards."

Christopher's mouth was dry. He paused for a sip of his tea, and then continued.

"The bottom line is this," he added. "If labor costs as a percentage of sales are growing faster than your profit margin, you know you are heading down the wrong path. It's not sustainable in the long run. The U.S. auto industry pays among the highest manufacturing wages in the world. Compared to Japan and France, the U.S. auto industry pays 50 percent higher wages and over five times more than Mexico's auto manufacturing facilities."

"It's no wonder so many jobs are going overseas," Mr. Carman interjected.

"Benefits are a factor too," Christopher continued. "When a union plant shuts down, whether it's for a week or a year, the union employees still get paid to the tune of 95 percent of their normal pay. Simply put, the hourly union benefits are far superior to those of the salaried worker. There's no equality. And we expect our entire workforce to work together to achieve great results with all these underlying issues? It's an outdated business model, pure and simple.

"On the issue of commitment, surveys show that the UAW members consistently identify more with the UAW than with the Ford Motor Company itself—even though we pay them. Often, UAW employees will tell Ford managers, as well as people working for them, that they don't work for Ford but they work for the UAW. Again, it's a shirts-versus-skins mentality, although on the surface it seems like Ford and the UAW are doing well together. The only way we at Ford seem to have good labor relations with the UAW is to yield to their demands."

"However, I do want to be clear in pointing out that most UAW workers are loyal employees of Ford," Christopher added. "Unfortunately, they are working under a contract that doesn't motivate them to operate any differently than they are, so it does not do either side justice."

Mr. Carman turned to Christopher, his piercing blue eyes looking directly into Christopher's.

"For Pete's sake! It's time to be fair!" exclaimed Mr. Carman. "You cannot continue to subsidize overinflated

UAW salaries and benefits at the expense of being competitive in the marketplace. There should be equality for all workers with a fair distribution of compensation, accountability, and sacrifice!"

"Management and labor seem to operate independently rather than in concert," said Christopher. "Shouldn't we all be operating under the same umbrella and with the same benefits?"

"You raise a great question, Mr. Hope. Perhaps I can shed some light on the matter," the lady offered. "You know, when my husband was alive, I traveled extensively around the nation, visiting relief projects, surveying working and living conditions, and then reporting my observations to the president. I was fortunate to exercise my own political and social influence. I became an advocate of the rights and needs of the poor, of minorities, and of the disadvantaged. I participated in the League of Women Voters and joined the Women's Trade Union League. I have always championed humanitarian causes.

"Besides wearing many hats as an author, political activist, columnist, teacher, diplomat, and First Lady, I was also a worker and a union member. What you are telling me is very disturbing indeed. I spent my entire life as a champion of workers around the world. I was eternally grateful for the generous support of the men and women of the labor movement. They valued my support and friendship. They worked with me in completing the Universal Declaration of Human Rights and as delegate to the United Nations in 1948. From my first meeting with the Women's Trade Union League in 1919 until 1962, I always quoted the AFL-CIO slogan—'One of us.'"

Christopher took notes, writing at a furious pace, wanting to record every word the lady said.

"I've had close and positive working relationships with union leaders, union members and especially union women, and with those seeking social justice and human rights in the workplace at home and abroad," stated the woman. "Working in partnership, we overcame barriers of class, race, and gender. I truly believed that what I did on a national and international level, everyone could and should do on a local level. Where, after all, do universal human rights begin but in small places, close to home, in the everyday world of human beings, the neighborhoods they live in, the schools or colleges they attend, the factories, farms, or offices where they work, where every man, woman, and child seeks to have equal justice and opportunity, equal dignity without discrimination? Unless these rights have meaning there, they have little meaning anywhere. Without concerted citizen action to uphold them close to home, we shall look in vain for progress in the larger world. I understood the world I lived in, because it belonged to me. The world you live in belongs to you and your contemporaries. I cannot judge your actions based on circumstances of another time. But to conclude my thoughts, Christopher," continued the lady, in a reprimanding tone, "it is quite evident that power and greed have corrupted the focus and mission. Many who have come before you sacrificed greatly for the freedoms and rights you have inherited today. Your generation bears a great responsibility. Inspired and accountable leadership is indispensable, especially during trying times, and it seems that your generation is being tested."

"That's part of the demise. We have not had a truly inspiring leader running the Ford Motor Company in over twenty years, except for the promise of our new leader, Alan Mulally," explained Christopher.

The lady placed the bouquet of roses on her lap, and her soft and nostalgic mood disappeared. She tightened her lips and straightened her posture.

Mr. Carman began to cough, and once again his breathing had become difficult. Albert appeared and served Mr. Carman another hot cup of soybean tea. Mr. Carman settled down and the lady continued.

"In my days, the labor conditions for workers were something that people in your time would consider criminal and third world. My advocacy for the union and for human rights covered basic human dignity and survival. It was hard-lined because of the greed of the employers and the lack of basic human requirement for food, shelter, warmth, safety, security, and compensation. In your world, the union has taken the wrong direction, moving away from its responsible purpose to protect the basic rights of the common man, and has become a political tool for greed, empowerment, and manipulation. I would have never supported such an atrocity of justice. This is not the America that my husband and I loved and served with complete trust and conviction. The union exists to protect and defend the weak, not to hold the company hostage. Wake up, my beloved America, before it's too late!"

A shroud of embarrassment and remorse fell over Christopher. He felt a sense of collective responsibility. He searched his mind for answers and solutions.

"The creation and approval of a realistic Ford contract that will allow flexibility to each in an ever-changing market without overburdening either party is the responsibility of both Ford and the UAW management. The UAW management in conjunction with Ford has endangered the entire future of the Ford Motor Company with the last deal they agreed to," explained Christopher.

"The solutions seem simple to me," observed Mr. Carman. "Employees should work side by side and learn to respect each other more. Ford's production line workers should be allowed greater latitude to perform different tasks. Ford should encourage and reward workers to find more cost-effective and better ways to assemble cars and trucks. Ford should continue to improve safety in our plants and make jobs less tedious. The company needs to chase out costs that rivals don't have to pay!"

"Each side has a big stake in cooperating with the other right now," added the lady.

"If the boat sinks, we all go down together," quipped Mr. Carman.

"You're both absolutely right. Either side has the potential to destroy the Ford Motor Company," said Christopher.

Mr. Carman looked directly at the lady seated beside him and said:

"Your acceptance of my invitation to Fairlane Manor means a great deal to me. I am grateful and delighted you came. There is also a personal reason that I asked you to come here today. Many years ago I had opposed issues that you and your late husband had advocated, such as the New Deal, and as you very well know, I have had my own strong disagreements with the UAW and other issues during my lifetime. I too had a dream to run for the highest office in the land and to lead our great nation, but I quickly discovered that a political career is like breakfast at the Coliseum. No one escapes the cruelty of the beast. I've always said that history was bunk. Why? Because historians write the supposed facts many years and even centuries after the heroes or villains are gone. Historians, in my opinion, are basically fictional writers, slanting, filtering, and spinning the so-called facts. Values and principles are eternal and can never be compromised. They stand the test of time."

Christopher nodded in agreement. Mr. Carman continued. "And I have faced my destiny for the choices I've made during my lifetime. Those who are entrusted with the responsibility to lead others will be held accountable for their decisions and judged accordingly. If I have been offensive to you and others during my lifetime, or caused harm to any one in any way, I ask forgiveness for being such a fool. Because in the final moment, when the mortal clock is silenced, on whatever side of the picket line we stand here on earth, we will be held accountable for our thoughts, words, and actions, to the ultimate CEO of all creation. Madam, you are an outstanding example to workers everywhere of selfless leadership devoted to the well-being of others. Please give my very best regards to the president."

The fire burned even brighter now, cracking and spewing embers onto the floor. The lady reached out her hand to Mr. Carman and placed it on his, in a gentle embrace. They looked into each other's eyes and smiled. Then the lady lowered her head to smell the roses.

It was time to go.

Christopher said good-bye to the lady who was escorted off by Albert into a Model A that had been waiting for her at the front entrance. Christopher took his raincoat from the cloakroom and headed toward his car, which was also waiting for him outside the gates.

"I'll see you tomorrow then," Mr. Carman told Christopher, waving good-bye from the front porch, "and remember,

FORD should stand for Focusing On Responsible Decisions!"

CHAPTER FOUR

Globalization—Forsaking the Homeland

The highest use of capital is not to make more money, but to make money to do more for the betterment of life.

—*Henry Ford*

The week was quickly passing by. Christopher had made a list of the topics he had hoped to cover before Mr. Carman departed for his journey abroad. He wondered if Mr. Carman would invite another friend over for lunch today and, if so, who the mystery guest would be.

As usual, Mr. Carman was waiting for Christopher on the porch, sitting in the rocking chair. Next to him, in the other chair, was a man of worldly distinction. The two men were engrossed in an animated conversation.

Mr. Carman and his friend waved to Christopher as he walked up the stairs toward the porch.

"I'd like you to meet one of my closest friends. He grew up near Dearborn, on around ninety acres of some of the best farmland in these parts," explained Mr. Carman. His friend smiled warmly at Christopher and stood to help his buddy from the rocking chair.

The man was tall and handsome. He had a perfectly manicured mustache and broad, chiseled features. His brown hair was neatly combed to the side. He wore an impeccable brown three-piece vested suit of the same old-fashioned style

Christopher had become accustomed to seeing in the company of Mr. Carman. He spoke with a cultured accent and in a reassuring tone.

"Come on, ol' friend, let's get out of this damp weather and go inside by the warm fire," suggested the man as he walked arm-in-arm with Mr. Carman into the dining hall. Albert took everyone's raincoats and hats and placed them in the coat room. The towering old grandfather clock chimed seven times, but Christopher didn't bother to check his watch today.

As Albert served lunch, Christopher took out his notepad and pen, and the conversation began. Immediately, the conversation led to the topic of globalization. Christopher was again amazed at the uncanny knowledge of Mr. Carman. Christopher had hoped to discuss Ford's recent tunnel vision on the subject of globalization. As he had expected, Mr. Carman had clear thoughts on the subject and had brought a friend who could lend further, much-needed insight.

"My buddy here," said Mr. Carman, "was the founder of one of the first global corporations in America and was an important contributor to North American economic growth in the twentieth century. You could say that his products have covered countless miles and have quite a track record. We have made many business and personal alliances over the years. We were members, along with another friend of ours who you met a few days ago, of a club that made us privy to exclusive business opportunities within our group. We could call each other in from any location and ask permission to purchase a building or other items on our word alone. We didn't even need a handshake."

"Ah! Such relationships rarely exist in the business

world today," said the man with a look of nostalgia coming over him.

Mr. Carman motioned to Christopher and invited him to get the conversation rolling.

"So tell me, Christopher," Mr. Carman said, "since we have my dear friend here who was on the cutting edge of globalization for our country, how is Ford handling global opportunities today?"

"Well," said Christopher, not sure where to begin, "I guess you could sum up Ford's take on globalization by saying that the Ford Motor Company has forgotten to make the main thing the main thing!"

"Well, what do you mean by that?" Mr. Carman asked, sounding intrigued.

"Yes, do tell," his friend prompted.

"Well, just to give you a little background, approximately 75 percent of Ford's revenue comes from sales in North America," said Christopher. "In that respect, in my opinion, we spend far too much time, energy, and resources trying to create a global empire and, in doing so, slight our focus on the cash cow business of North America. We constantly have our eye on trying to develop our next superstar foreign market. In turn, these foreign markets wind up becoming cash drains with no potential for profitability for ten to twenty years."

"What would be the sense in that?" challenged Mr. Carman's friend. "The very purpose of globalization would first and foremost be profit, would it not?"

"Well, it seems that our ego drives us into certain foreign regions," said Christopher. "In some of the regions, Ford initiates ventures where profitability isn't even on the radar screen and perhaps even impossible. Year after year, we lose revenues in markets such as Ford South America, Ford

Taiwan, Ford Japan, Ford India, Ford Thailand, Ford Russia, Ford China, and others," explained Christopher. "It's a fact that we sell more vehicles in an American city the size of Dallas than we do in some entire foreign marketplaces. That should show us that our global expansion strategies and business model should be a lean structure, driven only to expand sales and production at a profitable level.

"Instead, currently we have elaborate, overstaffed overseas operations, each with their own vice presidents and general managers. I suspect that the main drive for having these operations is not in the least the opportunities they afford top executives to visit or live abroad."

"You don't say," said Mr. Carman. "What a shameful excuse for lack of profitability!"

"Exactly!" trumped Christopher. "What we need to do is look at every potential market for opportunities to sell excess from our current worldwide production. Initially, we should establish a tight organization in a new market which offers minimal sales and service support to export products until the market can be established to support a full-service sales operation.

"We need to do a better job of evaluating potential export markets and establish a system to project return on investments for one year, five years, ten years, and longer. If cash is tight and we can't project profitable business from a venture within ten years, we need to set aside our ego and make a good business decision to opt out of that market. We need to resist the temptation to go to a future hot-spot market just because the competition is there or is going there."

"Now, you're making sense!" said Mr. Carman's friend.

"At present, the Ford Motor Company is facing a twenty-dollar-to-one-dollar labor disadvantage trying to compete in Asian countries against Asian labor," said Christopher. "At that rate, we also have to evaluate what the current demand is for our products today and what it could be by doing some basic marketing. For example, sometimes the demand for American-made medium and large vehicles and trucks is strong, but we try to force the sale of small vehicles into emerging markets, which compete at a cost disadvantage against Asian rivals. The whole proposition becomes unprofitable. The marketing loss of this strategy erodes any profit that would be made by the other segments. We end up in an unprofitable position just to have a presence in the global market, which creates more cash flow drains on the corporation. It is time to reevaluate and restructure every market we are currently doing business in and those we are planning to do business in. And if it doesn't make sense—don't do it!

"We also need to consider partnering with low-cost producers to develop products locally using their capital and our name, and leverage their low-cost production advantage with our Ford name and marketing expertise. While this may not be popular with the UAW, we must look at the options. And we also need to consider the import model used to create production facilities in the United States. The strategy is always the same. They request grants, no-interest loans, and subsidies from federal, state, and local governmental agencies. Sometimes they even get the land at no cost. So their start-up costs are 25 to 30 percent cheaper than U.S-based companies. Using the same approach abroad would help us. Some of these potential foreign partners for Ford would even be willing to offer medical subsidies to bring employment to their area. Global production and marketing may offer opportunities to grow the Ford Motor Company, but it should only be pursued if it is going to be profitable for everyone involved.

"You recall the brainy brand management decision to replace one of the world's most recognizable symbols, the Ford Oval, with the scripted Ford Motor Company? That decision cost us hundreds of millions of dollars. This was done to make us look more encompassing and more global—when, in fact, we make the vast majority of our money in the United States," continued Christopher.

"The Ford brand was and is one of the most recognized brands in our country and around the globe," exclaimed Mr. Carman. "Don't they know that the world is round and not an oval? Christopher Columbus figured that one out centuries ago."

"Once you break your brand and send out a message of instability and unreliability, you break your trust with people. The Ford Motor Company must not embrace the theory of 'If it ain't broke, break it!' with the blue oval," said Christopher.

Mr. Carman was visibly upset.

"Globalization, while a fair strategy for business growth, cannot exceed good business judgment in the rate of growth," said Christopher. "Standardization of platforms is good and allows a consistent growth strategy to globalize. Research must be executed thoroughly before making decisions as to where to go next with your product. Evaluations should be made based on return on investment and cost to establish a profitable venture—not just the annual profit and loss. More time needs to be spent analyzing new or emerging markets as well as major competitors.

"The Ford Motor Company has partnered with many companies as part of its globalization strategy, but profits and returns on investments haven't followed. Most of our partnering ventures, such as the ones with Volkswagen, Mazda, and Fiat, soaked up cash like an empty sponge. Then, just when it seemed like there was a light at the end of the tunnel, the light was really the tail lights of the companies with which we had partnered. They took our technology, the cash we invested in them, and then severed their relationship with us, leaving us holding the bag. Some of the foreign partnerships could have never made a profit, and some people say they were entered into because the Ford family and senior management just wanted to see the Ford logo as they vacationed abroad. Of course, now they won't admit that it doesn't make sense and they don't want to give up. Other times it seems like foreign projects are created because one of our competitors is there and it becomes a keeping-up-with-the-Joneses syndrome. Globalization draws millions of dollars out of profitable markets to have the opportunity to lose money abroad on every vehicle we sell. This does, however, justify many company-paid vacations abroad for senior managers, all the while driving up the cost of vehicles in our profitable markets and making it more difficult to sustain long-term profits domestically."

Mr. Carman grew pale. He shook his head from side to side in disbelief.

"This is completely unacceptable!" exclaimed Mr. Carman.

"European engineers have spent decades perfecting small vehicles that sip gas and are far more refined than the typical American economy box," Christopher continued. "Why not import some of these great cars from Europe to North America? Ford really needs to operate as a boundary-less global company that melds the strengths of all of its far-flung operations."

"I have a question for you, Christopher," interjected Mr. Carman's friend. "We use these terms 'global' and 'globalization' in so many contexts and questions. How would you define 'globalization' from today's point of view?" asked the man.

"That's a challenging question, sir," Christopher answered. "'Globalization' is a term used to refer to the expansion of economies beyond national borders—in particular, the expansion of production by a firm to many countries around the world. 'Globalization' also refers to the process of manufacturing and/or marketing products around the world, such as in the 'globalization of production,' or the 'global assembly line.' The concept of globalization has given transnational corporations power to reach beyond nation-states. Some critics today say that it has the potential to weaken any nation's ability to control corporate practices and flows of capital, set regulations, control balances of trade and exchange rates, or manage domestic economic policy. One of the concerns of the UAW is that globalization has weakened the ability of workers to fight for better wages and working conditions from fear that employers may relocate to other areas," explained Christopher.

"So, you are saying, that like many concepts, globalization of today has the power to make companies more successful, but it also can bring with it many complications that must be considered," said Mr. Carman.

"That's a fair assessment indeed," agreed Christopher.

"In my opinion, globalization presents many challenges, but I believe there is a very important overall benefit that comes with it," Mr. Carman's friend added. "Globalization of products leads to global cultures, where various traditions and backgrounds merge and blend, bringing different views, new ideas, and strengths together. America in itself is a model example of the benefit of the globalization of cultures. Our country has thrived from being a melting pot of various cultures. In fact, it could be said that our greatness lies therein. We have inherited this great nation from the sacrifices of hard-working people from all walks of life and cultures. It was they who built our railroads and highways and gave their lives for our freedom. The American Dream was born out of the great benefits of the globalization of cultures. The American Dream is the belief that through hard work and determination, any U.S. legal immigrant can achieve a better life, usually in terms of financial prosperity and enhanced personal freedom of choice. This Dream has always been a major factor in attracting immigrants to the United States. According to historians, the rapid economic and industrial expansion of the United States is not simply a function of being a resource-rich, hard-working, and inventive country, but it's the prospect that anybody can get a share of the country's wealth if he or she is willing to work hard. So, you see, it is my belief that most of the time, globalization can be a very good thing."

Mr. Carman nodded in agreement.

"Regardless of what country or environment we were doing business in," Mr. Carman added, "I could walk through the front door of any of our factories and out the back and tell you if it was making money or not," added Mr. Carman. "I could just tell by the way it was being run and by the spirit of the workers. Fairness and honesty should be the fundamentals of globalization."

Christopher paused for a moment, thinking to himself. Then, he replied, "A company's globalization strategy also requires a different skill set from domestic business, taking into consideration different factors such as tariffs, exchange rates, and important rules and regulations that apply specifically to corporations conducting international business. You have to weigh carefully the advantages and disadvantages among staying a domestically focused business and venturing into the global arena. And, as your friend wisely pointed out, the cultural factors in doing international business are huge. To attempt to be successful, you must approach new markets like a cultural ambassador, listening to how they think and feel, rather than imposing what you think is right. Many a business today would still be standing if they understood this simple lesson."

Mr. Carman's friend turned to Christopher.

"Christopher, I've had an incredible life and managed to take with me some important things I've learned along the journey. I'd like to share a principle of mine with you, and please remember to share this with others. The growth and development of people is the highest calling of leadership. Whether we are doing business domestically or aiming to become a global giant, remember that it is only as we develop others that we permanently succeed."

His simple and candid words penetrated truthfulness into the heart of Christopher and into the heart of the problems facing the Ford Motor Company and the American Dream.

It really didn't seem to matter anymore to Christopher if this mystery guest was really the famous inventor Christopher thought he was. There was a far greater purpose for this incredible journey he was on, and he was determined to follow its path to the very end.

Then Mr. Carman asked to be excused and to end the lunch earlier today. It was obvious that the news about the changing of the Ford Motor Company brand had deeply disturbed him.

It was time to go.

Christopher's eyes followed the shadowy figure of Mr.

Carman's friend as he slowly vanished down the long hallway toward the entrance of the manor.

"I'll see you tomorrow then, same time, same place," Mr. Carman reminded Christopher, "and remember,

FORD should stand for **F**ocus **O**n **R**esponsible **D**istribution!"

Albert walked with Mr. Carman to a room down the hallway, and Christopher let himself out of the manor. Looking through the thick beveled-glass widows out over the porch, he could see flashes of lightning and a thunderstorm approaching. He had almost forgotten to fetch his raincoat from the cloakroom. His car, as usual, was ready for him, perfectly parked in the front of the manor, keys in the ignition and with a full tank of gas.

All the way home, Christopher reflected on his conversation on globalization with Mr. Carman and his friend. *What we really need*, he thought, *is a nonbiased, centralized source that evaluates all our products and opportunities in new markets. We need to look at the demands of our markets individually and the cost of marketing all our products and make decisions as to which products go where. Products must be streamlined to a universal specification and built to the level that allows flexibility in marketing.* He would remember to include these thoughts into his notes of today's conversation as soon as he got back to his office.

CHAPTER THREE

Recapturing the Vision!

Failure is the opportunity to begin again more intelligently.
—Henry Ford

The fog hung heavy over the highway, and it looked like it was going to rain. As Christopher approached Fairlane Manor, he noticed two vehicles parked outside the gates.

One was an official-looking, unidentified black limousine with dark-tinted windows. An American flag flew on the side of the car, and the license plate at the back read "U.S. Government—Official Business."

The other vehicle wasn't a car at all. It was an American World War II high-ranking army tank. Mr. Carman was not sitting on the front porch today as he usually was.

Albert arrived at the entrance of Fairlane Manor to greet Christopher.

"I suggest you hurry on in, Mr. Hope. Mr. Carman's guest today is here on official business and is on a very tight schedule. Your meeting today will be brief and held in the library down the hallway. I will be serving a light lunch in there," instructed Albert.

He took Christopher's raincoat, quickly placed it in the cloakroom, and beckoned Christopher to follow him as they hurried down the dark hallway.

They arrived in front of two soaring mahogany doors, and Albert knocked three times.

Mr. Carman opened the door and motioned for Christopher to enter.

The library's walls were stacked with books up to the ceiling that soared at least twenty feet. The room was filled with many antiques and objects from different parts of the world. There was a long library table in the center of the room where books, maps, diagrams, and papers of all sorts were neatly piled. On a small antique side table, Albert had placed a tray with soybean tea and sandwiches.

Standing at the end of the table was a wall of a man wearing an officer's uniform. The first thing Christopher's eyes fixed on were the numerous medals and decorations on his jacket, the four stars and one he immediately recognized as the Purple Heart. Christopher's eyes moved up to the pipe dangling from the man's mouth. Then, before Christopher could think or breathe or say anything, the imposingly handsome man in an officer's uniform walked toward Christopher and reached out his hand, which nearly crushed Christopher's in his grip. Christopher felt an electrical energy charge right through him.

"I'd like you to meet my friend, the General," said Mr. Carman.

"Come on in, young man. Roll up your sleeves. We've got work to do. The company is in urgent need of a strategic restructuring plan."

Mr. Carman looked at Christopher, and a boyish grin flashed color across his pale face.

"You know what Will Rogers used to say: 'Take the diplomacy out of war and the thing would fall flat in a week.'"

Laughter broke out but only for a brief moment, and then the seriousness of the meeting had set in.

Spread across the oval library table was a detailed chart with graphs and writing on it.

There was an easel placed next to the table with a pointing stick.

The General had a long scrolled document under his arm. He unrolled it and clipped it on the easel.

"Young man, I suggest you get out your paper and pen and start writing your notes," he ordered Christopher.

"Time is of the essence, and in order to save the Ford Motor Company and the American Dream, a restructuring plan has to be devised and executed.

"There are obviously many problems to address. But at the core of the matter, in our analysis, the Ford Motor Company's leadership functions as an empire with the notion of divine powers over the people it is entrusted to serve. To reverse these downward trends, and prevent the impending collapse of this once-upon-a-time great American icon, we must march forward to democratize the Ford Motor Company and implement a strategic plan that will reestablish responsible leadership in the Ford Motor Company and serve as a model plan for every single corporation in America," outlined the General.

"Let me share some of my leadership experiences during our last world war, and perhaps we can learn some lessons on how to turn things around. Immediately after the Japanese announced their decision to surrender, I was appointed the supreme commander for the Allied Powers to oversee the occupation of Japan. Although technically I was under the authority of an Allied Powers commission, I took my orders from Washington. Rather than establish an American military government to rule Japan during the occupation, I decided to employ the existing Japanese government. I issued several direct orders to Japanese government officials but allowed them to manage the country as long as they followed the occupation goals developed in Potsdam and Washington. I realized that imposing a new order on the island nation would be a difficult task, even with Japanese cooperation. It would be impossible for foreigners to dictate radical changes to 80 million resentful people. Historians may judge my U.S. occupation policies as very harsh.

"But we could not simply encourage the growth of democracy. We had to make sure that it grew. Under the old constitution, government flowed downward from the emperor—who held the supreme authority—to those to whom he had delegated power. It was a dictatorship to begin with, a hereditary one, and the people existed to serve it. Sound familiar?" asked the General, looking directly at Christopher.

"Yes, sir, it sure does," answered Christopher.

"Remember that absolute power corrupts absolutely and that the basic keys to success are always the same," explained the General. "If the Ford Motor Company and others, who have surrendered to the enemy of greed and pride, follow the steps outlined in this strategic restructuring plan, they can be liberated once again, back on the road to freedom and success, simply because they have chosen to do the right things."

The General pointed to the chart on the board and read each item out loud. Mr. Carman stood proudly by the General's side while Christopher took down the notes.

The All-Star Restructuring Plan
*For the Ford Motor Company, Corporate
America, and Global Partners*

- Establish individual accountability at all levels—top to bottom.

- Tie compensation to productivity and contribution at all levels—consistently balanced.

- Make decisions based on logic and in the best interest of the company and employees. Decisions made on the basis of political correctness will never be profitable.

- Treat everyone equally, fairly, and honestly based on democratic principles.

- Do not discriminate against anyone.

- Ensure that managers are servant leaders—not self-serving leaders. That was how the Ford Motor Company was founded.

- Hire and promote based on a person's ability to contribute.

- Recognize that realizing potential means nothing unless performance outweighs potential.

- Value loyalty and consistent contribution as a top priority at Ford.

- Make decisions by listening to the Voices:
  The Voice of our Customers
  The Voice of our Dealers
  The Voice of our Employees

- Provide consistent and stable leadership at all levels and minimize turnover for the sake of change.

- Relaunch a system that provides feedback and compensation for people who provide ideas on reducing costs, improving efficiency, and growing market share. As cost and other improvements are realized, employees should be rewarded.

- Align products flawlessly to customer demands to maximize market opportunities.

- Value every employee's uniqueness and their contributions to the Ford Team with motivation and recognition programs.

- Replace worshiping diversity with honoring and leveraging the uniqueness of every employee.

- Focus on the automobile business and stay out of unrelated social issues.

- Ensure that all workers are motivated to perform and share in compensation, benefits, and risk, equally contributing and sacrificing as team members.

- Focus on the basics—don't exhaust resources looking for quick fixes.

- Million dollar solutions won't solve billion dollar problems.

- Return to the American values upon which the Ford Motor Company was founded.

- Maximize economies of scale when designing and purchasing.

- Maximize recognition and minimize waste.

- Take pride in being an American automobile company.

- Remember that process and systems provide structure and consistency—but people produce results.

- Hire, reward, and recognize rainmakers, not order takers and news reporters.

- Find more ways to leverage technology.

- Minimize unnecessary employee relocations that cause defections and drive up relocation costs.

- Develop and embrace leaders at all levels.

- Decentralize as much as possible, and empower employees with responsibility and accountability.

- Ignore trying to create a perfect Ford Portrait and focus on creating a healthy environment for everyone that values results, teamwork, respect, and diversity.

- Base employees' evaluations more on results they effected by actions taken and less on uncontrollables.

- Foster an environment where realistic goals and objectives are established and achieved.

- Have fun again and rejoice as you celebrate success along the way every chance you get!

Mr. Carman began to pace back and forth, with a renewed energy and optimism.

"I have also done some research and found, in discussing with former company employees, that we are on the right track," said Mr. Carman. "This message must immediately be communicated back to the Ford family and company leaders. They have to listen to the Voices around them, respond to them accordingly, and then do the right thing. They must be able to spend as much time as it takes to make decisions the right way. This has always been my firm belief!" concluded Mr. Carman.

There was a knock on the door, and Albert entered, holding the General's raincoat and hat.

"General, it's time to go. You are expected at headquarters in one hour," said Albert.

"Good luck, young man," said the General to Christopher. "And remember, patience, courage, and determination is the winning strategy. Follow this plan and Ford will return to greatness."

The three men marched down the hallway toward the entrance. Christopher noticed that a bright white light surrounded the General, a light so blinding that Christopher had to cover his eyes with his hands. When he removed his hands from his face, the General had disappeared.

It was time to go. Christopher took his raincoat from the cloakroom.

"I'll see you tomorrow then, same time, same place," Mr. Carman told Christopher, waving good-bye to him from the front porch, "and remember,

FORD should stand for Focusing **O**n **R**eversing **D**ownward trends!"

All along the drive home, Christopher was sorting out the information in his mind to organize for the media stories.

Then his cell phone rang. It was his friend, Frank McIntyre.

"Hey, Chris, did you get the reprint of last year's news article about Ford that I dropped by your office?"

"Yes, I did, and thank you, Frank. I should have called you back sooner, but you wouldn't believe the week I've had. I've got some great news for the feature you're working on about Ford right now. I think there's a way Ford can reverse these downward trends. Let's check our schedules and set a time to get together and find a way to share this hope with the public. Sure thing, talk to you later."

Frank couldn't believe his ears. It sounded like Christopher was about to give him the scoop of the decade on the Ford Motor Company. And best of all, it sounded like a positive direction for the company.

Walking toward the elevator doors in the parking garage back at the Ford Motor Company's headquarters, Christopher remembered he had forgotten something in his car and went back to retrieve it. As he bent down over the passenger side seat to get his papers, he noticed something fall out of his raincoat inside pocket. Lying on the floor was a white envelope. He took a second look at his raincoat and realized that it was not his coat at all, but Mr. Carman's raincoat. He had taken it from the cloakroom by mistake. It was Christopher's name, however, that was handwritten on the front of the envelope. In the upper left-hand corner were the initials HF. Christopher smiled. He hurried toward the exit stairs, deciding the elevator would be too slow. He couldn't wait to read what was inside. Seated at his desk, he opened the letter. The note was personally written and in a familiar tone.

From the Desk of
HF

April 6

Dear Christopher,

It's been great! I think you're on the right track and I'm impressed with your willingness to hang in there. We need good people like you to stay and help turn the company around. Thanks for investing the time with me. I enjoyed getting up to speed at what is going on at Ford. It does seem that the environment has changed drastically since I founded the company.

I'd like you to organize your notes and share them with my family and the people currently in charge of the company. But remember, however, that the basic keys to success are the same as we discussed. Explain to them that there needs to be individual accountability, compensation tied to productivity, and a balance between business and political correctness. Ford must return to an atmosphere where everyone is treated equally and where no one is discriminated against for any reason.

At Ford, managers have to become servant leaders, not self-serving leaders. These truths were what our company was founded on. We paid a premium price for employees when we started the company, but we demanded a premium day's work. Regardless of race, gender, or ethnicity, we put everyone to work with the same pay and expected the same amount of work out of them. I think that if Ford is going to be successful in the next century, the company is going to have to focus not only on the potential of an individual, but on their ability to contribute and produce in today's global marketplace.

While we do have some seasoned Veterans, we also need to listen to the Voice of our Customers, the Voice of our Dealers, and the Voice of our Employees. We need to relaunch a system that provides feedback and compensation for people to provide ideas, and incentive programs with recognition. Incentive programs must provide motivation to all employees and encourage them to give us their best ideas and performance.

We need managers to be true leaders, with the ability to listen, respond, and do the right thing.

As the founder of the Ford Motor Company, I am grateful to all who have stayed the course. To them, I say, keep working hard with loyal conviction and a commitment to bettering the lives of our fellow man. I pray that God will continue to bless this great country and the Ford Motor Company and keep the American Dream alive.

I will be leaving tomorrow for my journey abroad, but I will be at Fairlane Manor in the morning, preparing for my trip. I have some last-minute things to arrange, some work on the generator, and instructions for Albert. I'd like to invite you to be my guest at the manor one last time. Why don't you drop by with your notes and join me for a cup of soybean tea?

Sincerely yours,
Henry Ford

Henry Ford! Christopher knew it! He did not understand how the meetings of the past week had taken place, but somehow, he knew he wasn't meant to know. He was thankful that he had been granted such an incredible opportunity and acutely aware of the responsibility of the mission. Now Christopher had to attend to the task of carrying Henry Ford's message.

That evening, Christopher stayed up till dawn, typing all the notes and the All-Star Restructuring Plan. The messages were clear, powerful, insightful, truthful, and hopeful. He signed off the notes, in his usual style, with a historical quote of wit and wisdom. The company could turn around if it would listen to the Voices, follow the plan, and realign to the values evident in Henry Ford's original vision.

Christopher hadn't slept a wink that night. It was about 5:00 a.m. He went to the kitchen and made himself a hot cup of herbal tea, quite out of character for him since he had been a coffee addict as far back as he could remember. He smiled to himself, sipping the hot brew and looking outside the kitchen window, watching the sun rise over Dearborn. *I guess you can teach an old dog new tricks*, he thought.

Christopher then remembered a book he owned since college—a historical collection profiling the lives of the twentieth century's greatest inventors. As if in a daze, he walked into his study and stood in front of the wall of books above his desk. *It's got to be here somewhere*, he thought, his eyes searching across the bookshelves. And then he spotted it on a shelf right in front of him. He removed the book from the shelf and sat down at his desk to read it. Christopher scanned the index looking for the chapter on Henry Ford. Flipping through the pages, his finger stopped on what he was searching for—the events on the fateful day when Henry Ford died. After Christopher finished reading, he closed the book. He understood. It was time to go.

CHAPTER TWO

The Messenger

Chop your own wood, and it will warm you twice.
—Henry Ford

When Christopher left for Fairlane Manor the next morning, the springlike April day that had arrived at his doorstep only a few hours earlier now felt more like a cold October day as the skies filled with rain clouds and the winds swayed even the sturdiest of oaks. Christopher hummed a song he had remembered from church that Sunday: "Will those that come behind us find us faithful?" It seemed to be a recurring chorus that he just couldn't get out of his head.

The closer he got to Fairlane Manor, the worse the weather became. It had been like that from the first day they met. There, rocking on the porch and reading a book, was *Time* magazine's Man of the Century himself, Henry Ford.

Christopher's heart was racing. It's hard to explain the emotions that Christopher was feeling that morning. Mr. Carman was indeed Henry Ford, the farmer, inventor, the common man, the *real car man*, and the founder of one of the greatest companies in the world to work for. Christopher was determined, but he was also worried that he might not be able to deliver the message to those who needed to get it. His ability to relay the message to the Ford Family and the company was not completely in his own hands. They had walls of assistants blocking direct access. It would be a challenge. He also

169

knew now that Henry Ford's cough was more than a cold. Sadness came over Christopher.

"Mornin', Christopher," said Henry Ford, who was rocking in his chair on the porch.

Christopher glanced down at the book on Henry Ford's lap. It was *Walden* by Henry David Thoreau. Today, Henry Ford was casually dressed in overalls and a worker's cap. An old farm tractor, whose engine was running, was parked at the side of the road.

"Mornin', Mr. Ford. So . . . you really are a 'car man'!" exclaimed Christopher excitedly, his face beaming with pride. Christopher held his breath, waiting for Henry Ford to say something.

Henry Ford smiled and winked at Christopher, his eyes twinkling.

Christopher held Henry Ford's raincoat neatly folded over his arm.

"I seemed to have taken your raincoat by mistake, Mr. Ford, my apologies," offered Christopher, placing it down on the railing.

"So you have, young man," said Henry Ford with a glint in his eye.

Henry Ford seemed peaceful today, and he wasn't coughing anymore. There was a glow about him—a certain light emanating from him.

At that moment, Albert came out of the manor carrying Christopher's raincoat and a tray with a pot of piping-hot soybean tea and three cups and saucers. He placed the tea tray down on the wicker table and handed Christopher his raincoat.

"Thanks, Albert," said Christopher.

Albert smiled and walked back inside the main house.

"Mr. Ford, I found the letter you wrote me. It fell out of the pocket of your raincoat. I stayed up all night and summarized the notes from our lunch conversations," explained Christopher, handing Henry Ford a large envelope.

"Here, sir, is the true story about the Ford Motor Company. I have included your letter to me and the strategic All-Star Restructuring Plan for the future of the Ford Motor Company. Thank you, Mr. Ford, for listening to me and for coming back."

"Much appreciative of your help as well, Christopher," Henry Ford replied. "And I have one more thing for you. It's a personal letter from me to those at the Ford Motor Company. It might come in quite handy when you try to get the Ford Family and the leadership to listen to you."

Henry Ford handed Christopher a letter-sized white envelope that was carefully tucked in the pages of his book. Christopher sat down in the rocking chair next to Henry Ford and waited while Henry Ford read Christopher's notes. When Henry Ford had finished reading them, he looked over at Christopher and smiled. He was obviously pleased.

"Well done, well done! Thank you for taking such care to record my message for Ford's future. Now, why don't you go ahead and read that letter that I just gave you? I hope you will do everything in your power to communicate my message to those who need to hear it."

Christopher read the letter. When finished, he looked over to Henry Ford and said, "I'm already on the case, sir, and as a matter of fact, Mr. Ford, I hope you don't mind, but I took it on myself to invite, so to speak, someone from the company here to meet you this morning," said Christopher. "He may just be the next leader who can carry the Ford Motor Company forward with the same values and principles the company was founded on."

At that very moment, Alan Mulally, the chief executive officer of the Ford Motor Company, pulled up to the front gates of Fairlane Manor in his F250 Crew Cab. When Mulally got out of his truck, he looked curiously around him, noticing the old tractor parked on the side, and the lineup of antique cars—a Model T, a Model A, an Edsel, a T Bird, and a Mustang in the parking lot—an incredible display of all of the famous Ford cars throughout its history.

Henry Ford carefully observed Mulally as he walked up the steps of Fairlane Manor. He stood perfectly still with his chin up and his arms folded in front of him. Christopher was almost certain he could see tears welling up in Henry Ford's eyes.

Mulally looked surprised and caught off-guard.

"What's going on here, Hope?" Mulally asked, approaching the landing of the porch.

Mulally had been to Fairlane Manor numerous times before for business luncheons and special events, but today everything looked completely different, he thought.

"Your department didn't brief management that this was going to be a special event with period props. I was told that our company was holding a press conference today at Fairlane Manor at noon, on the day of the anniversary of the death of Henry Ford. Actually, I spent most of the morning at the Henry Ford Museum researching more on the life of Henry Ford, trying to get a better sense of the man, getting some inspirational quotes and preparing a positive statement about the future of the company," explained Mulally.

Just then thunder erupted and lightning jolted the sky. A misty rain began to fall.

Mulally looked around the grounds and then said: "Strange . . . you know, when I left the Henry Ford Museum on the way here, the weather suddenly began to change. It got real foggy and the winds almost rocked my truck off the road," Mulally remarked. "My cell phone didn't work, and my car radio went wacky on me—the only thing I could get was a scratchy old

Ford commercial from fifty years ago. Did somebody from your department mess with my radio? And what happened to this place? It's been remodeled or something. The cars, the old tractor—why it looks like new, and this man looks exactly like Henry Ford! It's quite a commendable effort to recapture the look and feel of a time gone by. What a great idea, Christopher! But I don't see any media trucks. Where's the press? Who else do you expect? Are we on time?"

"Well, Mr. Mulally, you are just in time. There is no one else coming, only you," explained Christopher. "Today is the anniversary of Henry Ford's death, April 7. He died tonight, exactly sixty years ago, here at Fairlane Manor, at 11:15 p.m., with his wife Clara Bryant Ford and his maid, Rosa Buhler, at his side. There is no press conference happening here today, and this man, who looks like Henry Ford, is, in fact, the real car man himself, Henry Ford. The press conference idea was the best way I could get you here today and away from your busy schedule."

Mulally's smile quickly faded.

Albert came back outside and approached Henry Ford with some news.

"Mr. Ford, the power is completely out now and the generator has stopped working and the telephone is dead. You can't stay too much longer."

"I know, Albert. Just a few more minutes, please."

Albert nodded.

Henry Ford turned to Mr. Mulally and smiled.

"Welcome to Fairlane Manor, Mr. Mulally. I've been expecting you. Would you like some soybean tea?"

Mulally then noticed the third cup and saucer on the tea tray. Albert gave a cup to Henry Ford, a cup to Christopher Hope, and then a cup to him. Mulally was beginning to understand that his invitation to Fairlane Manor today was providential.

At that very second, the old grandfather clock chimed one fateful single chime. The winds picked up, bending the branches of the large old oak, and the rain fell heavier. Mulally glanced down at his wristwatch—the hour hand was stuck at seven. *It should be noon,* he thought.

"What time do you have, Christopher?" inquired Mulally. His wristwatch was his only link grounding him to reality. Christopher looked at his watch.

"Well, in present time it should be noon, but in history, where we are, it's seven o'clock. It's the seventh of April, Mr. Mulally."

Mulally stood still, barely blinking, and barely breathing. He had prided himself on his logic, keen sense, and analytical ability, but there was another side to Mulally that his family and friends knew well—the dreamer, the adventurer, the visionary, and the spiritual man. He looked directly at Henry Ford, who smiled warmly at him and offered him his hand.

Mulally gazed a few moments at Henry Ford, his hand still in Henry's, and seemed to begin to come to terms with who was standing before him. Christopher noticed a gleam beginning to sparkle in Mulally's eyes. Mulally was buying into it and wasn't sure why. It just felt right. He knew he was supposed to be there. He knew this from the first day he became the leader of the Ford Motor Company.

"You know, Mr. Ford," said Mulally, "when I stopped at the Henry Ford Museum on the way over here today—walking through the rooms and exhibits, I felt different—excited and energized. I felt like a youngster again, wanting to explore, invent something, and discover something new and different. I felt happy and confident."

Henry Ford nodded and then replied: "I always said that when you can't handle events, let them handle themselves. And you know what Will Rogers once said—'Even if you're on the right track, you'll get run over if you just sit there.'"

Henry Ford's signature humor always seemed to have perfect timing. He knew how to bring people together.

"You have been my all-time hero, Mr. Ford," remarked Mulally. "And I want you to know that I take seriously and respectfully the responsibility of my leadership and my accountability to you and the principles you founded the Ford Motor Company on," Mulally continued, his voice lowering to a whisper and his thoughts drifting as the incredible encounter with history began to really sink in.

"As you can imagine, Mr. Mulally," replied Henry Ford, "I can't stay much longer. This is the day I left many years ago, but it seems like only yesterday. It's funny how everything changes, yet everything remains the same. Tried to get that generator Edison gave me to work, but to no avail. Got pneumonia from this nagging cough that I just couldn't kick. I knew there was trouble down here so I came back for a visit. I was fortunate enough to come across Christopher Hope— who has been meeting with me every day for the past week. He has a sincere interest in seeing the company turn around. Christopher has told me quite a bit about the company's present-day condition, many things which perhaps you may not be aware of just yet. In turn, I have shared with Christopher my perspective on how I think company leaders should respond going forward. This company was founded on my vision, yet I realize that another true company leader could take that vision, tailor it, and carry it to the next level. From what Christopher has told me, you could just be the person to do that. Please take the time to read the notes that Christopher has prepared from our meetings and relay my message. You'll know what to do."

Alan Mulally stood face to face with history and face to face with himself.

Christopher reached out his hand to Henry Ford for a final good-bye.

"Sir, you introduced me to some of the most important people to have ever walked the earth, who came back to set the record straight," remarked Christopher, "and I will always remember everything you shared with me. I promise to communicate the message that the future of the Ford Motor Company and America relies on our ability to return to the basic values and principles this company and our country were founded on," said a misty-eyed Christopher.

Henry Ford smiled and shook Christopher's hand, patting him on the back. And then he turned to Mulally.

"Sometimes, Mr. Mulally, in order to go forward, you have to go back. As Will Rogers used to say—'Rumor travels faster, but it don't stay put as long as truth.' There is a difference between having your name on the back of a check as an employee and having your name on the front of the check as the one responsible for funding all those checks. My name is still on the front of every check, and I take that very seriously! And my signature is on every vehicle you make, right in the center of the oval. Oh, and in case they haven't figured it out yet, tell them that the world is not an oval, it's round!"

Mulally smiled and nodded in agreement.

The three men sat down in the rocking chairs. Christopher handed Mulally his copy of the notes he had typed, and Henry Ford and Christopher sat quietly and waited while Mulally read them through. When Mulally turned the last page of Christopher's notes, he looked directly at Henry Ford and said, "You know, often when you look in the mirror, it doesn't always look good and sometimes the truth hurts. But it's important that we take the time to look in the mirror and see where we really are so we can be honest with ourselves."

Mulally read through the notes once again. On the very

last page, Christopher had signed off the document with an inspirational quote of wisdom. It was by Booker T. Washington, and it read:

Success is to be measured not so much by the position that one has reached in life as by the obstacles which he has overcome.

Mulally was quiet and reflective. He seemed to have lost track of time, and when he looked up toward the rocking chair where Mr. Ford had been only a few minutes before, it was empty. Mulally glanced over to Christopher who was leaning on the porch's railing and waving off into the distance.

Looking out over the porch toward the entrance of Fairlane Manor was Henry Ford sitting high up in his old tractor. He waved back to Christopher and Mulally and called out, "Hey, fellas, I just might check back with you from time to time to see how things are going in the future!" With a final tip of the hat and a wave of the hand, Henry Ford slowly drove away, meandering down the winding road and disappearing into the distance.

The parking lot was empty now as all the antique cars had disappeared. Rays of warm sunlight broke through the clouds and shined down on Fairlane Manor. Mulally looked at his watch, which was now working fine, and the time said it was noon on the button. Albert was gone, and everything looked new again.

Christopher reached into his raincoat pocket and took out the envelope that Henry Ford had given him only moments ago. He handed it to Mulally.

"There is one more thing I'd like to share with you, sir. Henry Ford handed this to me before leaving on his journey and had asked me to give this to you. It's written on his personal letterhead and signed by him."

Mulally's heart raced. His hand slightly trembled as he opened the doors of history and read the handwritten letter signed by Henry Ford.

From the Desk of
HF

April 7

To Whom It May Concern,

I thought I told you everything you needed to know, but you didn't listen. I told you time and time again but just didn't listen.

I started this company and founded it on certain values. I gave you the values and principles that I lived my life by. You left them. You abandoned them. I gave you the vision and principles to ensure your success—you lost your focus. I anticipated this might happen if you didn't listen or learn. I thought you understood that money has never solved problems, it only reveals character. You have lost touch with reality and with the people you are privileged to serve.

Please read the notes which Christopher Hope has recorded for you from our conversations. Take them to heart and act on them. They will help realign your vision and get you back onto the road of success. I am certain that the Ford Motor Company will make it if we get back to the basics. We have always done the right thing.

Oh, by the way, if you are still looking for the other $20 million of mine that nobody's found yet, well, here's an excellent incentive and compensation for a well-earned reward.

Before I passed on, I gave those $20 million to a trustee to invest, more than eighty years ago. Today, it's worth an estimated value of over $100 billion. I had anticipated that this might happen in the future, so I created this account. I have given the trustee information to Christopher Hope, for the future of the Ford Motor Company.

You know what Will Rogers used to say—"Don't gamble. Take all your savings and buy some good stock and hold it till it goes up, then sell it. If it don't go up, don't buy it."

Sincerely yours,
Henry Ford

Mulally carefully folded the letter and placed it into his jacket pocket.

He walked over to Christopher who was still leaning on the porch railing looking out into the distance down the road where Henry Ford had been only moments before.

"How did you meet him?" asked Mulally.

"He found me on the road, my car was dead, I was stranded, lost, and had absolutely no direction. Then he rescued me. Sounds crazy, doesn't it?" said Christopher.

Mulally put his arm around Christopher's shoulder, and the two men looked out from the porch far into the distance.

"Well, Christopher, it just might take some crazy ideas and a lot of hard work to turn our company around!"

As they looked out over the beautiful gardens of Fairlane Manor, the rain stopped and a majestic rainbow reached out across the clearing skies. In the far distance, they could see Ford's world headquarters right under the rainbow. Christopher Hope and Alan Mulally looked at each other and smiled.

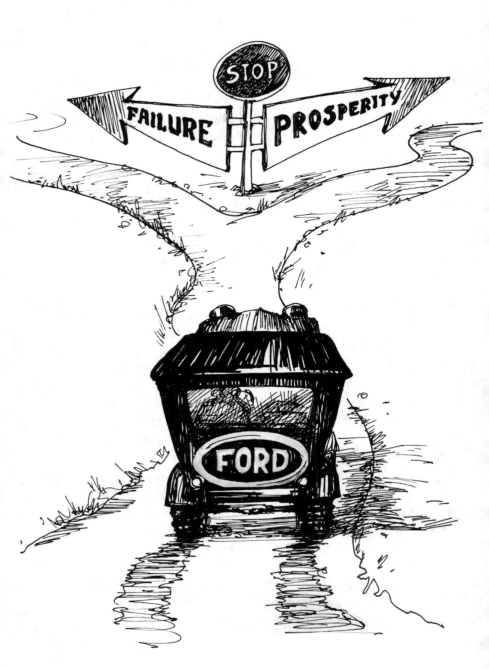

CHAPTER ONE

Roadmap to the Future

Failure is the opportunity to begin again, more intelligently.
—Henry Ford

The All-Star Restructuring Plan
For the Ford Motor Company, Corporate America, and Global Partners

- Establish individual accountability at all levels—top to bottom.

- Tie compensation to productivity and contribution at all levels—consistently balanced.

- Make decisions based on logic and in the best interest of the company and employees. Decisions made on the basis of political correctness will never be profitable.

- Treat everyone equally, fairly, and honestly based on democratic principles.

- Do not discriminate against anyone.

- Ensure that managers are servant leaders—not self-serving leaders. That was how the Ford Motor Company was founded.

- Hire and promote based on a person's ability to contribute.

- Recognize that realizing potential means nothing unless performance outweighs potential.

- Value loyalty and consistent contribution as a top priority at Ford.

- Make decisions by listening to the Voices:
    The Voice of our Customers
    The Voice of our Dealers
    The Voice of our Employees

- Provide consistent and stable leadership at all levels and minimize turnover for the sake of change.

- Relaunch a system that provides feedback and compensation for people who provide ideas on reducing costs, improving efficiency, and growing market share. As cost and other improvements are realized, employees should be rewarded.

- Align products flawlessly to customer demands to maximize market opportunities.

- Value every employee's uniqueness and their contributions to the Ford Team with motivation and recognition programs.

- Replace worshiping diversity with honoring and leveraging the uniqueness of every employee.

- Focus on the automobile business and stay out of unrelated social issues.

- Ensure that all workers are motivated to perform and

share in compensation, benefits, and risk, equally contributing and sacrificing as team members.

- Focus on the basics—don't exhaust resources looking for quick fixes.

- Million dollar solutions won't solve billion dollar problems.

- Return to the American values upon which the Ford Motor Company was founded.

- Maximize economies of scale when designing and purchasing.

- Maximize recognition and minimize waste.

- Take pride in being an American automobile company.

- Remember that process and systems provide structure and consistency—but people produce results.

- Hire, reward, and recognize rainmakers, not order takers and news reporters.

- Find more ways to leverage technology.

- Minimize unnecessary employee relocations that cause defections and drive up relocation costs.

- Develop and embrace leaders at all levels.

- Decentralize as much as possible, and empower employees with responsibility and accountability.

- Ignore trying to create a perfect Ford Portrait and focus on creating a healthy environment for everyone that values results, teamwork, respect, and diversity.

- Base employees' evaluations more on results they effected by actions taken and less on uncontrollables.

- Foster an environment where realistic goals and objectives are established and achieved.

- Have fun again and rejoice as you celebrate success along the way every chance you get!

And remember:

FORD should stand for

Focusing **O**n **R**ight **D**etails!

Focusing **O**n **R**ight **D**ecisions!

Focusing **O**n **R**ealistic **D**ecisions!

Focusing **O**n **R**ealistic **D**esigns!

Focusing **O**n **R**esponsible **D**iversity!

Focusing **O**n **R**ewarding **D**eliverables!

Focusing **O**n **R**esponsible **D**ecisions!

Focusing **O**n **R**esponsible **D**istribution!

Focusing **O**n **R**eversing **D**ownward trends!

Founded **O**n **R**ight **D**ecisions!

From the Desk of
HF

April 7

Dear Mr. Mulally,

Don't be afraid to be proud that we are an American company founded on American values. The benefits of that will always outweigh the costs.

I believe that in dark times in history or in life, poor decisions have a way of repeating themselves, unless a light shines on them.

And one last thing before I go. Throughout my life I have found that real leaders base their decisions on their core values rather than public opinion and that way they don't have to keep changing their decisions and Ford Motor Company was founded on right decisions!

Sincerely yours,
Henry Ford

Author's Note

We are extremely indebted to the current and former Ford employees and their families for their years of service and loyalty and the sacrifices they and their families have made. The Ford Motor Company has always relied and will continue to rely on the best automotive retail network in the world—the Ford and Lincoln Mercury dealers. We wish to thank them and their families for their unwavering loyalty to Ford. We will continue to need them to regain leadership in a growing, competitive market.

Our suppliers have always provided us with a unique partnership opportunity. You have always made Ford look great and stood with us along the way.

The Ford Motor Company's future will also be greatly impacted by the current and future employees who will surely be tested by a rough sea and ever-changing work environment. The company's future may be uncertain, but the outlook is good for a long-term turnaround. The success will rely on your loyalty, patience, creativity, and willingness to work with our partners to share in the cost and the reward of future success.

We will need every member of the Ford team doing their best. America is relying on all of us to save the American Dream. This story is not only about the Ford Motor Company but it is about thousands of American companies who find themselves in the same predicament as Ford does today.

And remember:

Future Opportunities Rarely Develop
without all of us winning!

CL

About the Authors

CLIFTON PETER LAMBRETH has worked for the Ford Motor Company for over twenty years in a variety of positions. Clifton has been a rainmaker at every position he has held and has consistently been a top performer throughout his career at Ford. He has received prestigious awards and distinctions, including five Ford Inuksuk Drive for Leaders Awards and has won three Diversity Leadership awards. Clifton has been a Ford College recruiter for over ten years at Cornell University, University of Pennsylvania, Johnson Business School, and the Wharton Business School. He graduated from Thomasville Senior High School in North Carolina, having been a proud alumnus of the North Carolina Baptist Children's Mills Home. He went on to receive his BSBA in marketing and management and his MBA from Western Carolina University. He serves on the board of directors of the Family Foundation Fund, on the advisory board of Lead Like Jesus Foundation, as well as the advisory board for Western Carolina University's School of Business. As CEO of Daniel Bradley Matthews Inc., he provides strategic automotive and marketing consulting. Clifton is a public speaker and author. He enjoys competitive running and he has run the Marine Corps Marathon, Philadelphia Marathon, and Boston Marathon, and competed in over 150 5K and 10K races. Clifton has three sons and lives with his wife Susan and family in Brentwood, Tennessee.

MARY HELEN CALIA'S professional career in investor and public relations spans over twenty-five years. Mary graduated from Grover Cleveland High School in Queens, New York; attended Manhattan Community College; and has two certificate degrees in biomedical sciences and graphic arts. She began her career at the Hospital for Special Surgery in New York City, where she worked on research publications and was given an honorable mention in the *Journal of Bone and Joint Surgery*. She cofounded North America's first full-service investor relations firm—Marcel Knecht & Associates Inc., servicing more than five hundred public companies since 1982, including Alcan Aluminum, Power Corporation, and others—and received numerous business awards for high ethical standards and innovation. Mary launched Europe's first IR firm in Paris, France, and has provided counsel to emerging growth companies, Fortune 500 CEOs, and political and industry leaders. She was featured in the *Nashville Business Journal* as one of America's top businesswomen and some of her prominent communications clients include Congressman Marsha Blackburn, Kline Preston Law Group, and others. Mary has served on various boards, including the Montreal Neurological Hospital and the Jewish General Hospital. She has been recognized for her historical contributions in the art world including the placement of the first sculpture by an American realist artist into the Hermitage Museum. She is a public speaker, author, and composer. She has four sons and lives and works in New York City and Brentwood, Tennessee.

MELISSA LEIGH WEBB is a freelance writer and publicist in the Nashville area and is a correspondent for several local newspapers. She handles public relations for numerous prominent clients in the Nashville area. Melissa graduated Magna Cum Laude from Mississippi State University in 2002, having earned dual bachelor's degrees as part of the International Business program with emphases in marketing and German. She completed an internship with Nabisco Inc. and participated in a study abroad program in Vienna, Austria. Melissa worked as an associate marketing manager and training consultant for Lane Home Furnishings in Tupelo, Mississippi. During her time at Mississippi State, Melissa served as chapter president of her sorority, Zeta Tau Alpha. She currently serves on the board of directors for the Spring Hill Chamber of Commerce, the Spring Hill Imagination Library, and the Spring Hill Kiwanis Club. She is also Vice Regent of the Tenassee chapter of the Daughters of the American Revolution. Melissa and her husband, Emmett, live in Spring Hill, Tennessee.

About the Artist

IGOR BABAILOV, MFA, is one of the most sought-after artists of our time. Recipient of numerous awards, Babailov received his master of fine arts degree from the prestigious Surikov Academy. His works are in museums, galleries, and private collections worldwide. He has painted officially commissioned portraits of world leaders, celebrities, and social, business, and political elite, including Pope John Paul II (Vatican Museum); Pope Benedict XVI (Vatican Museum, under way); President George W. Bush (Presidential Collection); America's mayor, Rudolph Giuliani (Giuliani Partners, NYC); President Vladimir Putin of Russia (the Kremlin); Prime Minister Brian Mulroney of Canada (Parliamentary Gallery); President Nelson Mandela of South Africa (Presidential Collection); Senator Hillary R. Clinton (Clinton Presidential Library); Byron Janis (Steinway Hall Museum); Bob Costas (Joe DiMaggio Collection); filmmaker Akira Kurosawa (Starlight Starbright Foundation, Japan), and others. *New York* magazine featured Babailov as one of America's top artists. He serves on several distinguished boards, including the Child Art Foundation in Washington D.C., and is an exclusive speaker of the Harry Walker Agency of New York. See www.Babailov.com.

PRESS RELEASE

This Year Marks 60th Anniversary of Death of Henry Ford as the Company Embarks on a Path unlike any other in the Company's History

For Immediate Release: Detroit, Michigan, April 7... Today we remember the loss of a great man. Henry Ford passed away on this day sixty years ago.

Henry Ford was famous for founding the Ford Motor Company, but the positive impact his life had on society reaches far beyond the automotive industry. Henry Ford changed America through the simple genius upon which he founded his company. As the first to pay minorities and women equal pay for equal work, he was the ultimate defender of human rights with a vision to improve the quality of life for the common man.

Ford's Model T was the chief instrument leading to one of the greatest and most rapid changes in history in the lives of common people. The original Ford cars were made for and by everyday Americans. Ford factories provided jobs that paid a living wage, leading to the evolution of the middle class in America. The Model T relieved rural farmers of isolation. Eventually, the invention of the automobile and its accessibility to the majority of Americans allowed cities to spread outward, creating suburbs and housing developments. Millions could go wherever they pleased. Henry Ford's vision transitioned American society from the agricultural era into the industrial era.

Time Magazine's Man of the Century, Henry Ford, continues to provide solutions for the Ford Motor Company today, even beyond the grave.

"I believe that the Ford Motor Company can return to the heights of its great historical accomplishments," said Christopher Hope, Vice President of Public Relations for Ford. "We can achieve this through retrospection and introspection that will allow us to again find the roots that have made us strong for all these years. With a new leader at the helm, we have the opportunity to forge ahead. Henry Ford provided the ultimate roadmap to success for Ford. By returning to the principles of his vision and values, the Ford Motor Company can once again take its position as a global leader in the automotive industry and the American Dream will continue."

Source: Ford and the American Dream Public Relations